CONTROL YOUR
DIVORCE
THE QUESTIONS TO ANSWER

CONTROL YOUR
DIVORCE
THE QUESTIONS TO ANSWER

Jody Beveridge and Jan Bennett
MA Barrister at Law   LLB (Hons) Solicitor

foulsham
LONDON • NEW YORK • TORONTO • SYDNEY

foulsham

The Publishing House, Bennetts Close, Cippenham,
Slough, Berkshire, SL1 5AP, England

ISBN 0-572-02856-3

Printed in Great Britain by Creative Print and Design (Wales), Ebbw Vale

CONTENTS

Acknowledgements 6

Introduction 7

Chapter 1 Exploding Common Myths About Divorce 9

Chapter 2 Answers to the Most Commonly
Asked Questions 23

Chapter 3 Choosing and Meeting a Solicitor 33

Chapter 4 The Grounds for Getting a Divorce 43

Chapter 5 A Step-by-step Guide to the Divorce Process 53

Chapter 6 Mediation 67

Chapter 7 Money Matters 71

Chapter 8 The Children 103

Chapter 9 Domestic Violence, Injunctions and
Occupation Orders 121

Chapter 10 Living Together 131

Chapter 11 Notes on State Benefits and Child Support 137

Chapter 12 Personal Stories 145

Glossary 180

Useful Addresses 184

Index 189

ACKNOWLEDGEMENTS

The authors would like to thank the following people:

Carol Jessop, Debbie Fenby, Helen Boynton, Jenny Smith, Nicola Barnard, Frances de Graff, Nikki Ball and Jan Leopard, Eeva and Francis Beveridge, Martin Dunn and Simon Sykes; and Shirley from the Women's Aid National Domestic Violence Helpline.

We would also like to thank the editorial team at Foulsham for their never-ending patience and encouragement! Special thanks to Wendy Hobson and Amanda Howard for all their support and hard work.

And finally thank you to all those people who talked to us about their personal experiences of divorce for the purposes of this book.

INTRODUCTION

If you have picked up this book because divorce is on your mind, then it's likely that either you yourself, or someone close to you, is going through a very difficult and confusing time.

You probably have a thousand questions that need answering. You may not have much idea how the divorce process works, how decisions are made about money matters or where the children should live. You may never have been to see a solicitor, or even know whether a divorce is definitely what you want. If that is the case, then this book is designed to answer some of those questions.

In writing it, we have assumed that you don't know much about what getting divorced means, and we have tried to answer in as simple language as possible many of the questions we are asked on a daily basis. Our aim has been to keep the book free of legal jargon, and where that can't be avoided we have tried to explain the meaning in plain English.

This book is not designed for academics or lawyers; it is not a legal textbook, but it is for anyone who feels that, for whatever reason, he or she would like to know a bit more about the divorce process in England and Wales. (While England and Wales share the same laws and legal procedure, the law relating to divorce in both Scotland and Northern Ireland differs in some respects. Our advice, if you are thinking about a divorce in Scotland or Northern Ireland, is to find a book relating to the procedure in those countries.) We may not have covered all the points that are specific to you, because everyone's case is so different, but we hope that from reading this book you will gain a much better understanding of how decisions are made, and what would be likely to happen in your particular case.

What we cannot do is give advice on whether or not divorce is right for you. This book does not try to persuade you either way on that issue, as only you will be able to make that very difficult decision. We do hope, however, that that decision may be a little easier once you have found the answers to some of your questions.

The two authors of this book work in the field of divorce on a daily basis. Jan Bennett is a solicitor and Head of the Family Department at Askew Bunting Solicitors in Middlesbrough. Jody Beveridge is a barrister at York Chambers, working exclusively in family law throughout the north-east of England. Both of us have felt for some time that there are very few books available that tackle the issue of divorce in an informative but easy-to-understand format. Our intention is that this book will go some way towards bridging that gap.

In addition to the work we do in our professional lives, we have also both gone through a divorce ourselves, so we have some experience of being the person needing advice as well as being the person giving it.

If in reading the book you feel that you would like to contribute to a future edition or that there are subjects that could usefully be added, then please feel free to contact us via the publishers. We would be very interested to receive your ideas and feedback. We hope that you find this book useful, and wish you the very best in resolving whatever issues may be relevant to you.

Jody Beveridge and Jan Bennett

CHAPTER 1

EXPLODING COMMON MYTHS ABOUT DIVORCE

Question: How many divorced men does it take to change a light bulb?

Answer: No one will ever know because the wife always gets the house!

If you are either thinking about or in the middle of getting a divorce you can be sure that everyone you speak to will have something to say on the topic. They will either have been divorced themselves or know someone else who has … even if that someone is a character in a soap opera! Listen to too many of them and you will end up even more confused than when you started. As the joke above demonstrates, people have a tendency to generalise about what happens in 'every divorce', or else they spread completely wrong information about what a divorce entails and who has the power to make decisions. We've chosen some of the most widespread myths and rumours that we've come across from both clients and colleagues in order to dispel them right at the start!

> Rather than referring to he/she in every paragraph, we have tended to refer in each case to either the husband or the wife. There is no intention on our part to sound sexist, but it is nevertheless true that certain misconceptions are held more by men than women and vice versa. The answers apply equally to both husbands and wives.

As long as you have been married for a year, you can get a divorce if the marriage is not working out

Not quite true. It is right that you cannot file for divorce before you have been married for a year. However, you cannot get a divorce just by saying that you feel 'bored' or that you have 'grown apart', even after that first year has elapsed. You still need to show that there are grounds for a divorce, and in England and Wales these are:

- unreasonable behaviour
- adultery
- separation for two years if both people agree to the divorce
- separation for five years if one or other person does not agree to the divorce
- desertion (for a minimum period of two years)

See also Chapter 4.

The woman always gets the house

Not true! Be very careful about people who tell you what 'always' happens in a divorce, especially where money and assets are concerned. Every broken marriage leaves behind a different set of finances, so comparing someone else's to yours could be misleading if you don't have the full picture.

It is true to say that where there are children of the marriage, then whichever person is to look after them full-time has a better chance of getting the house. It is also true to say that more often than not it will be the mother who looks after the children full-time, but this is not always the case. It is important to remember that even if the wife gets the house, she must still be able to pay for any outstanding mortgage on it. If she can't do this on her income, the solution might be to sell the house and for both people to start again. In marriages where no children are involved, there is no automatic assumption either way as to who will get the house.

Frank and Jean

Frank and Jean had been married for over 30 years when Jean decided to file for divorce and moved in with her sister. At the time of the divorce, Frank was in his late fifties, but had not been able to work for several years since an injury at work had left him medically unfit. Instead, he did some casual work for a farm near his home, and kept pigeons in his back garden.

Their case was unusual, because when it came to making a list of the assets that had accumulated over 30 years, there was nothing to write down. The couple had no savings, no money and no assets. They had lived in the same house in a small village throughout the marriage and it was still rented from the local authority. The only thing left to argue about between them was which of them should keep the tenancy of their council house.

Jean's case was that she was only temporarily at her sister's and that she should have the right to move back into her home. She, too, claimed to have medical problems and said that the council had told her it would take up to six months for her to be rehoused. Frank, on the other hand, had very personal connections with his home. He was an active member of the neighbourhood watch scheme, did odd jobs for everyone in his village and had cultivated a vegetable patch in his back garden (along with his pigeons!). He was a very popular man in the village and several of his friends had written letters to the court saying how much they relied on him as an active member of the local community.

This was not an easy case, and one in which money played no part. Both Frank and Jean had lived in that house for a long time, and one of them would be faced with having to rehouse. Their children had grown up and left home so weren't relevant to the decision. Frank's doctor had produced a letter saying that he would be under severe stress if he was forced to move from his home. In the end, it was this factor that swung the case in his favour, along with the fact that Jean had already moved out and had somewhere else to live, albeit temporarily.

It was sad that after all that time together there was nothing left to split between the two of them, but in the end it was Frank who won the right to keep the tenancy of the marital home and he has carried on improving his vegetable patch ever since.

She won't be able to touch my pension

I've referred to 'she' here because it's mainly men who believe this one, and it's completely wrong. The law relating to pensions has recently changed and is relevant to all divorces except those where the divorce petition was filed before 1 December 2000. There is a lot to consider when it comes to pensions so we don't want to over-simplify it here (see Chapter 7) but it is now possible for a pension fund to be split to create two new, and completely separate, pension funds. Whether or not this happens will depend on whether the fund was built up during the time of the marriage, how much the fund is worth, how long it is until the benefits kick in, and what other assets there are available in the marriage. However, pensions (whether owned by the husband or wife) are a very relevant asset nowadays and often play a large part in deciding how the assets should be split.

I wasn't unfaithful because I had already separated from my spouse

Most of us think being unfaithful means having an affair when you are in a stable relationship with a partner, married or not. Many people think you can't be unfaithful to someone if you have already separated from them. Morally, that may be right. In divorce law, however, 'adultery' means having a sexual relationship with a person other than your spouse while you are still married to them. Whether or not you are separated is irrelevant so, for the purposes of a divorce, if one partner has been unfaithful at any time during the marriage, then this is a ground for divorce under the current law (unless you live together for six months or more from the date you discovered the adultery – see page 45).

Sarah's story

Sarah and Tom had been married for only two years but it was obvious that things weren't working out between them, so they decided to separate for a while and moved to live at opposite ends of the country. They also agreed that they were free to see other people if they wanted to.

Over the next couple of months they both had brief flings. Despite what they had agreed, when Tom found out Sarah had been seeing someone else, he was furious. She was astonished when a letter arrived saying that he was filing for divorce on the grounds of her adultery. To Sarah's mind, she had not even been unfaithful because they were separated and living totally separate lives, and Tom had his own girlfriend. The ironic thing was that by that time Sarah had begun to re-evaluate the marriage and would have been prepared to give it another go, but Tom wouldn't even discuss it. While Sarah was not happy about taking all the blame for the breakdown of the marriage, her solicitor pointed out that, at the end of the day, it was only a bit of paper and wasn't going to affect anything in the long run. Eventually, Sarah admitted the adultery and the divorce was concluded in about four months. Sarah still feels that they may have been able to save the marriage, but commented, 'You can't save it on your own, can you?'.

If the court has to get involved, everything will be sorted out within a week

Television is to blame for this one. If soap operas decided to portray court proceedings as they really are, then they wouldn't stay on air for long as the viewers would all die of boredom. What they do instead is to tell us in one episode about a legal problem, and then miraculously sort it out in court within a week! Custody battles have been settled almost overnight in *EastEnders;* a residence dispute in *Emmerdale* took place in the wrong court, with the wrong judge, with no legal representatives and no reports from family court welfare! They may make good viewing but none of these stories has any bearing on the truth. Soap operas are fun to watch but you can imagine how frustrating it is when a client comes into a solicitor's office saying that he or she wants something done because 'that's how they did it in *Coronation Street'*.

The truth is that any matter that proceeds to court (apart from emergency cases) will inevitably take time because there are steps to go through before a Final Hearing is even listed. Depending on why you are having to go to court, your solicitor will be able to advise you on how long it is all likely to take; however, you can be sure that it won't all be resolved within a week!

She won't let me see the kids

Again, this one usually comes from the husband who is not 'allowed' to see his children. It may well be the case that a wife looking after the children is angry about the separation and seems unwilling to discuss the husband's contact with the children. However, this is not the end of the story. Both parents have the right, if matters can't be sorted out in a friendly way, to apply to the court for an order that they should have contact with the children. One parent cannot just make the decision that the children won't see the other parent any more. In addition, a common misconception is that the mother is able to dictate the terms of contact for the other parent – for example, allowing the father to see the children only between 2pm and 4pm on a Sunday afternoon at McDonalds.

It's also common for mothers to say that the children cannot meet the father's new partner. As a general rule, the courts will not uphold any bar on meeting new partners provided that the introduction is done gradually, at a level that is acceptable to the children. If there are serious concerns that a child might not be safe with the other parent, then this is something that will be looked into properly by an independent person before any decision is made by the court (see Chapter 8). Otherwise, though, it is the general presumption that children have the right to grow up seeing both their natural parents.

If he doesn't pay Child Support then he can't see the kids OR she won't let me see the kids so I'm not paying Child Support

Both wrong. It may not seem fair that a father, for instance, can still see the children even if he does not keep up with Child Support. Equally it may not seem fair that a father has to keep paying even when he's having problems seeing the children, but the law is very firm on this. The courts view issues about children and money as being completely separate. An absent parent is under a duty to pay Child Support whether or not he sees the children. In addition, a parent has the right to see his children whether or not he is paying Child Support. Be careful not to confuse contact issues and money issues; the two are entirely separate.

She is not getting half the assets because she walked out on me

Another scenario that often does not seem fair. People think that if one party is to blame for the breakdown of the marriage, especially if they walked out, they should not be entitled to an equal split of the assets. The courts, however, do not see it in this way. The splitting of the assets is completely separate from how the marriage broke down. The emphasis in divorce has moved right away from blaming one person or the other. It is extremely rare for a court to be interested in whose fault the break-up was, and it is only in exceptional circumstances that a person's conduct will have any bearing on how the assets of a marriage are divided.

He isn't entitled to my savings/TESSA/endowment because they're in my sole name

Not true. As long as the marriage was not extremely short, the likelihood is that almost everything owned by both the husband and the wife will be viewed as a 'matrimonial asset'. What this means is that everything, whether in a sole name or in joint names, is considered to be the property of both, and is therefore relevant when you are looking at how the assets should be split following a divorce. The important point here is to tell your solicitor about all the assets you are aware of, whether in your name or your spouse's. A court has the power to order the transfer of an asset from one party to the other, whoever's name it was in originally.

The debt is in joint names but I won't have to pay it because it wasn't me who spent the money

Not true. Debts can often cause a problem following the break-up of a marriage because, unlike assets, the court does not have the power to remove a person's name from a debt. Regardless of who spent the money, if the credit card bill is in joint names, then the credit card company has the right to come after both of you for the money until the debt is paid. Along the same lines, if a debt is in your name only, then it is you the company will come after to pay it, and not your spouse. Debts can be taken into account in the financial split, however. If you are having to take on the matrimonial debts, then you may well be entitled to a larger share of the available assets.

He will get a better deal than me because he can afford to pay a solicitor privately

Not true. The quality of service you get from a solicitor has nothing to do with whether you are paying for it privately or the Legal Services Commission is paying for you. In fact, if you qualify for Legal

Aid, then you can only be represented by a firm with a 'franchise'. This means that it is properly inspected on a regular basis to make sure it is doing things properly. The firm has to meet certain standards in respect of client care, acting promptly, keeping you informed, etc. Although solicitors should meet these same standards even if they take only private clients, we strongly advise that, whether you qualify for Legal Aid or not, you look for a firm with a franchise, as then you will know that they will be checked to ensure they meet a minimum standard in their work.

If we have lived together for six months then everything will be split 50:50

We have to admit to being quite astonished at how widespread this particular myth has become, but we're reliably told that many people go to solicitors thinking that they have rights over the other person's property, having lived with him or her for over six months. This is completely wrong.

The concept of 'common law marriage' is a very misleading one indeed. Living with someone does not give you anything like the legal rights that you would have if you were married. Whether that is fair or not is another matter altogether, but under English and Welsh law, that is the situation. Living with someone for six months will not give you any rights at all over the other person's property; neither, in fact, will living with them for a much longer period unless certain factors can be proved.

This is a knotty area of the law, even for lawyers, so if you are in this situation and trying to make a claim on a house in someone else's name go to Chapter 10, where we have tried to explain the law as simply as possible. The basic fact, however, is that when there has been no marriage, the house belongs to the person whose name is on the title deeds, its legal owner. On marriage a house in one person's name can become a 'matrimonial asset' (the property of both people) but living together does not have that effect. If you have lived together and can show that you regularly made contributions to the mortgage or that you paid, for example, for substantial work to be done on the house, then you may have a claim for a percentage of the house's value (the equity), but this is not always straightforward.

He says that if I divorce him I'll get nothing

Forgive the implied sexism here, but the truth is that it's far more common for a woman to believe the above statement than a man, though of course it could happen the other way round. It is sometimes the case that when one spouse wants to file for divorce, the other can feel so strongly about it that they will threaten all sorts of things to try to stop it happening. Most commonly, wives are threatened with being left with nothing by their husbands, and this can be a very scary prospect if you don't know where you stand.

There is much more on this subject in Chapter 7, but for now the important thing to know is that is not possible for either spouse to make decisions about what the other will or won't get, and if he's threatening that you will end up with nothing, then he's mistaken. Every financial settlement is arrived at differently, depending on how much is available and the needs of each party, but no husband has the power to take all the assets and leave the wife with nothing. Whether you end up reaching an agreement as to how to sort out the finances or whether it's eventually done by a court, both spouses have rights. The essential thing is to get legal advice as to the relevant factors in your particular case, so that if you want a divorce and are scared of the financial consequences you can at least make an informed decision about whether or not you wish to go ahead with it.

She shouldn't have a share of the house because I've paid for it and she's never worked

This myth is often tied in with the previous one. People frequently think that if they are the sole breadwinner in a marriage, then they should have more, if not all, of the assets. This is not the case. The starting point in almost all divorces is that both spouses are considered to have contributed equally to a marriage. The fact that one stayed at home and didn't earn money does not mean that he or she has not contributed equally. Looking after children and looking after the home are just as important to the running of a family as going out to work and earning money. With today's rising costs of childcare, it is becoming more and more common for one partner to stay at home full-time, at least until the children are at school. It certainly would not be right for someone to be penalised financially at the end of a marriage for being a homemaker. In very rare cases it can be argued that one person did not contribute equally to the marriage, but this is only in exceptional circumstances and certainly would not be a runner just because one person had been at home looking after the house and the children.

Jackie's story

Jackie and her husband Geoff had been married for 19 years when they decided to divorce. They had two sons who at the time were 16 and 13. Geoff had a well-paid job; when they separated he was earning over £50,000 a year. Jackie hadn't worked since their eldest child was born – a decision she and Geoff had taken jointly. When they split she wasn't that bothered about money, but was determined to get the house to provide security for herself and the children. Geoff said she wasn't getting anything because she hadn't paid for it in the first place. Jackie felt he was ignoring the fact that she'd stayed at home to support him in his job, at the expense of a chance of a career of her own.

The house was valued at £69,000, with a small mortgage outstanding. They had a second property in Spain, which was worth about £25,000. They also had some savings and Geoff had a substantial pension. Although Jackie was advised that she had a good case to make a claim on the pension, especially as the children were staying with her, she still only wanted the house. However, Geoff wasn't prepared to agree to anything and even changed solicitors three times. It was 18 months from the grant of the decree nisi before the finances were sorted, mostly because of him wasting time with his solicitors.

Jackie tells her story in more detail on page 171.

He won't sign the papers so I can't get divorced

Not true! Once you have decided to go ahead and file for divorce, the next step is that your husband (or wife) is sent a copy of the divorce petition and a document called an Acknowledgement of Service that he has to sign and return to the court within 14 days. The reason for this is to prove to the court that he is aware that a divorce is in progress and has the chance to respond if he wishes.

Many people think – wrongly – that if a person refuses to sign this document, then that is the end of the divorce and you cannot proceed.

If you have a stubborn spouse (let's say the wife this time) who will not sign the Acknowledgement of Service then there are other ways to prove to the satisfaction of the court that she is aware of the proceedings without her having to sign anything. A bailiff will usually be sent round to hand over the documents to her personally. Once that is done, the bailiff is able to swear a statement saying that she has received the necessary papers. If she still refuses to sign, an application can be made to the court by your solicitor asking to dispense with the need for her to sign the documents. As long as the court is satisfied that she has received the papers, knows what is going on and simply does not wish to co-operate, then the divorce can proceed without her having to sign anything.

He/she won't give me a divorce

In part this myth is related to the one above. We've already explained how you can get round the problem of a spouse who doesn't want to sign papers. How about a husband (say) who will admit to having received the papers but doesn't want to admit what you allege as the grounds for divorce? Does he have to 'give' you a divorce for things to go further? The quick answer is no.

However, if you are filing for divorce on the basis of his adultery it can be a bit more tricky, because you do need an admission from him that he has committed adultery (unless you are able to prove his adultery without one). This can either be in the form of a statement that your solicitor will send him direct or on the Acknowledgement of Service as mentioned above. If he won't admit to it then a common way to get round this is to use the suspicion of adultery as one of the examples of his unreasonable behaviour, as under this heading you can proceed without any admission on his part.

If you have filed for divorce alleging unreasonable behaviour, then as long as a judge agrees with you that the behaviour you mention is unreasonable, the decree nisi will be granted. The only way your husband can stop this happening is by 'defending the divorce'. This means that he denies behaving in the way you claim he has, and must be prepared to come to court to have a hearing on whether he is guilty of unreasonable behaviour or not.

Cases like these are not at all common. Being realistic about it, if one of you is so determined to get divorced that you are prepared to go to court to fight for one, then that in itself is usually a pretty clear signal to the court that this marriage is not worth saving. The way round it for a husband who does not want to admit to what you have alleged is to 'consent to the divorce' without admitting any of your accusations.

If all this sounds a bit technical we hope it is better explained in Chapter 5. The important thing is not to worry if your spouse says he won't 'give you' a divorce. He doesn't have to!

I'll never be able to find out anything about his finances because he won't show me any of the papers

This is a very common fear among wives who think that their husbands will hide the true extent of their assets. Of course it is true that when it comes to divorce there are those who attempt to hide as much as possible about what they have, to try and prevent the wife from getting her entitlement, but this is not the end of the story.

Courts are well aware that this sort of thing goes on, which is why there are detailed rules about what each party in a divorce has to show to the court, including bank statements, pay slips, credit card bills, documents relating to insurance, savings, shares and pensions etc. Producing these documents is known by lawyers as 'disclosure'. If a husband refuses to disclose any of these documents (or in fact any other document related to the marital finances), he will be ordered by the court to produce them. If he carries on refusing to co-operate then the court can take steps to obtain the information directly from banks or employers. In the most extreme cases where someone does not co-operate with disclosure the court has the power to send him to prison.

The court also has the power to make what is called an 'inference' about any missing documents. What this means is that if important pieces of financial information are missing when the court is deciding about the finances, then a judge can make up his own mind as to what the missing information would have said, had the document been produced at court. People who are slow to disclose information are often attempting to delay the proceedings, and they often succeed. They should be warned, though, that deliberately concealing information or not sticking to court deadlines can result in very heavy penalties against them and is rarely worth the effort in the end.

Linda and Nigel

The problem with this case was that from the time Linda filed the divorce petition to the end of the financial hearing took just under four years. At least three of those years were wasted because of Nigel's refusal to comply with the court in disclosing his financial position.

Things started normally. Linda had a solicitor, but Nigel had chosen to represent himself. Both were directed by the court to file statements dealing with their finances by a particular date. Linda did so, but Nigel refused. The matter came back to court on several occasions and court orders were made against Nigel, but he stubbornly refused to obey any of them and he ignored all the letters from Linda's solicitors. It is not difficult to imagine how demoralising this whole process was to Linda, who was doing everything by the book.

About a year into the proceedings, because of information Linda had, Nigel was forced to admit that he had another property, which he had been hiding from the court. More delays occurred when the court ordered that this property should be valued because, once again, Nigel refused to co-operate and refused to answer letters. It was only when Nigel was threatened by the court with prison that he started providing the information. Further delays happened when he applied for various adjournments so that the Final Hearing had to be put back several times. In fact, perhaps thinking he was being extraordinarily clever, Nigel used every trick in the book to delay the final decision for as long as he was able.

On the one hand, Nigel's tactics worked; poor Linda waited patiently for four years until she finally got her fair share of the assets. On the other hand, however, he was left feeling a little less smug when after the Final Hearing Linda's solicitors applied for the court to make a ruling on the issue of legal costs. Once the judge had heard the whole story about Nigel's tricks, constant delaying tactics and refusal to co-operate throughout the four years, it didn't take long for him to decide that it would be only fair for Nigel to pay the vast majority of Linda's legal bill. Because of Nigel's behaviour, the huge amount of extra work that he'd caused, and the fact that the case had come to court on no fewer than 10 occasions, Linda's bill was astronomical and Nigel was ordered to pay just under £10,000. That money would have been far better spent shared between the parties than funding the legal profession. So, although some people still think that they can get away with not disclosing information to the courts, they should beware, because in the long run they might well have to face the consequences.

Conclusions

In this chapter you have read some examples of myths about divorce that you may have heard before or even believed yourself. There are hundreds more rumours that go round about divorce and everything that surrounds it, and often when one person is talking about his or her own experience, that story suddenly becomes the way all divorces are done. The important thing to remember is that no two divorces are exactly the same, so you can't always use someone else's story to predict what will happen in your own. Even seemingly minor differences can have a major impact on the end result.

The best thing you can do is to get as much information as possible about the process involved in getting divorced, and how decisions are made on the surrounding issues such as money and the children. Tell your solicitor exactly what your personal situation is, and then use the advice you receive to decide as to the best way forward.

CHAPTER 2

ANSWERS TO THE MOST COMMONLY ASKED QUESTIONS

In writing this chapter we started by writing down all the questions that our own clients ask us on a regular basis. We also asked many people who were either thinking about a divorce or had already been through the process exactly what questions they thought a book like this should answer. To be honest, we were surprised at some of the responses we received. Even those of us who deal with divorce on a daily basis sometimes forget that no two cases are identical. Each person comes with his or her own worries, concerns and misunderstandings about what getting divorced means. No book will answer every question, just as not every answer will be relevant to all who read it. In the end we decided to use this chapter for two purposes: firstly, to try and answer some of the questions that we are asked most often; and secondly, to choose some others that perhaps we hadn't thought of ourselves, but which people have asked us to cover. We hope that you will find something here of relevance to your situation.

How much will it all cost?

As we are sure you already know, lawyers do not have a reputation for providing a cheap service. However, for an ordinary bog-standard divorce with no complications surrounding the assets or the children, and allowing for variations depending on where you live and the solicitors you use, your average figure is likely to be somewhere in the region of £600. Then again, as you will see from the stories at the end of the book, legal costs can and do reach as much as £10,000 for a complicated case.

It is always worth asking your solicitor to give you an idea of the likely cost of your divorce at the beginning of the whole process, and also getting regular updates as to the current bill so you are not taken by surprise at the end. Some firms are prepared to give you a quote when you first make an appointment, but always be aware that this will change if any complications arise further down the line and the solicitor is required to do more work than expected.

You should also think carefully throughout the proceedings about whether there would be any chance of reaching a compromise rather than throwing away thousands in legal fees. Sometimes proceeding with a case in order to win a small amount can mean than you end up losing far more in costs.

How long will it take?

A straightforward, uncomplicated divorce is likely to be over in about four months. It is very unlikely, because of all the forms and paperwork that need to be filed, that the process can reach a conclusion any quicker than this. In a complicated matter where there are problems over children or money, the whole process can take a lot longer, sometimes years in extreme cases, though many efforts are made nowadays to resolve matters much more quickly than used to be the case.

If my spouse won't agree to a divorce, does that mean that I can't get divorced at all?

No, it doesn't mean that, though a divorce is undoubtedly a lot quicker (and cheaper) when both sides agree that it should go ahead. When one person won't agree to a divorce, then the burden is on the Petitioner (the person who starts off the proceedings) to prove that the grounds for a divorce exist.

A spouse who will not agree to a divorce can either choose to ignore all the paperwork completely or he can 'defend' the divorce, which means he fights the grounds on which you are trying to divorce him. Even if he ignores all the paperwork, as long as the court is sure that he has received the papers, knows about the proceedings and the grounds for a divorce exist then the divorce can still go ahead without his co-operation, though it will take slightly longer.

If, however, your spouse decides to actively fight the grounds you are relying on for the divorce, then it may be that you end up having a court case over whether or not the grounds for a divorce actually exist at all. For example, if you accuse your husband of adultery he might deny it and put the burden on you to prove to a court that this has in fact happened, which is likely to lead to quite a long delay before things are finalised.

This sort of case is covered in more detail in Chapter 5, pages 59–60.

How common is it for someone to defend a divorce petition?

Although it is quite common for spouses to start off by threatening never to allow a divorce to go ahead, in practice it is very unusual for a defended divorce to get as far as the courtroom. Usually the stubborn spouse will back down when he sees that you really are intent on the marriage coming to an end. Whether or not he is happy with the grounds of divorce you have chosen, there is rarely much point in trying to stay married when your spouse has made it clear that the marriage is over. Judges too are not usually in the business of prolonging marriages that one of the parties clearly does not want to continue, so your ex's legal advisers are likely to give him some pretty firm advice as to whether carrying on the fight will be worth his while in the long run.

What rights does my husband have to see the children?

In the majority of cases where couples with children split up, they are eventually able to agree between themselves how often the absent parent (the person not living with the children) should see them. Often this is a very informal arrangement, where the parents just agree a pattern of contact between themselves. Solicitors can also help with negotiating a contact arrangement, though sometimes the absent parent chooses to drift away from the children altogether.

Sometimes, though, contact cannot be agreed. Then your husband can make an application to the court for an order allowing him contact with the children (this is explained fully in Chapter 8). Briefly though, unless he has done anything so serious that the judge thinks it is in the children's best interests not to see him, he will normally be allowed to have contact with the children. The general view is that it is better for children to grow up knowing who their natural parents are, warts and all, unless this is clearly not in their best interests for some reason. You will not normally be allowed to stop the other parent having contact just because you don't like him any more.

If contact becomes an issue between you and your ex and goes as far as court, then a family court adviser will also be appointed to meet all those involved and make recommendations to the court as to the best outcome from the children's point of view, taking all the circumstances of the case into account.

Will I have to go to court in order to get a divorce?

If you have the grounds for divorce, and your spouse either admits those grounds or decides not to oppose the divorce, then you will not have to go to court over the granting of the divorce itself. However, you may still have to sort out issues concerning either money or the children. Again, if these matters can be agreed through solicitors or just between husband and wife, then you will not need to go to court. If you can't reach an agreement on one of these matters, then it may be that you will have to go to court for a judge to make a final decision on the matter.

Do I have the grounds for a divorce?

The answer to this question is explained in much more detail in Chapter 4 but briefly, to get divorced in England and Wales you must be able to show that you can prove one of the following grounds before you will be entitled to a divorce:

- that your spouse has committed adultery

- that your spouse has behaved in such a way that you cannot reasonably be expected to live with him or her (commonly known as unreasonable behaviour)

- that you have lived as separate households for two years and you both consent to the divorce OR that you have been separated for five years if your spouse does not consent to the divorce

- that your spouse has deserted you (and you have lived apart for at least two years)

If none of the above grounds for a divorce exists, can we divorce if I admit to being unfaithful with someone else?

No you can't. You can only use adultery as a ground for a divorce if you can show that your spouse has committed adultery against you, though of course your spouse could start the divorce proceedings on the basis of you being unfaithful with someone else if he or she wanted to.

Once I have visited a solicitor, do I have to go through with the divorce?

No you don't. Visiting a solicitor is not an irrevocable step at all, but often just an opportunity to find out what your options are. There is nothing at all to stop you taking some legal advice about your position and then deciding that you do not actually want to go ahead with a divorce.

If I admit there has been domestic violence, will someone come and take the children away from me?

Unfortunately we come across stories of domestic violence very frequently, but this question had not occurred to us as something that might worry a client until it was asked. It is never healthy for a child to be in a situation where domestic violence is happening, but social services are not in the business of removing a child unless the child is running a significant risk of emotional or physical harm. If you are a victim of domestic violence and trying to get away from that situation, or trying to get help, then it is highly unlikely that anyone will try to remove your children, as long as you, as their parent, are able to ensure their safety. The important thing is to do all you can as a parent to protect your children from any harm they might see or suffer as a result of violence within your home or relationship.

Will I lose my home?

There would be little point in trying to answer such a huge question in a single paragraph as every situation is so different and so many factors have to be taken into account. But the answer will depend on your and your spouse's housing needs, who the children are living with, whether you can afford to keep the house on your own, and whether it would be a fair outcome on your spouse for that to happen. It will also depend on whether the house you are in is just right for your housing needs or whether it is much bigger or more luxurious than you actually need it to be. See Chapter 7 for more details on housing.

How will all our money be split between us?

The starting point nowadays for the court (unless it has been a very short marriage) is that any split should be 50:50 between husband and wife. Don't count on that, though, as being the definitive answer. The actual percentage of the split can vary enormously depending on how much there is to go round, whether both people work and how much they earn, the needs of both husband and wife (for example, can they both rehouse themselves?), how old both husband and wife are, if there are children and, if so, who they are living with etc. To get a clearer picture of how agreements are reached, or in cases where there is no agreement how court orders are made, you should read Chapter 7.

My husband works abroad. How can I trace what he has and stop him from hiding all the money in the marriage?

We have to be honest and say that if one person in the marriage works abroad, this can make things much more complicated. If your husband is willing to tell you about everything he has there is not likely to be a problem, but if he tries to hide monies, assets or accounts, then things can get a little tricky. If you know that a divorce is likely, your best bet is to keep a copy of as many financial records and statements as possible. This might help even if you don't have the numbers of the foreign bank accounts because, if you can show (from bank statements) that cash is being withdrawn from an English bank account and then disappearing, at least this gives you the right to ask where the money is going, and your ex will be under an obligation to give you an answer. If he refuses, a judge can always be asked to draw his own conclusion as to what is probably going on, even though you can't prove it one hundred per cent.

If the financial side of things goes to court he will also have to prove his income through wage slips covering at least 12 months, and you should be able to see the statements for whichever bank accounts his wage is paid into. A court also has the power to order your ex to produce bank statements from any country; the difficulty comes if he refuses, as the court may not then be able to order the foreign bank itself to produce the documents you need. Remember, though, that if he refuses your requests the court can make up its own mind as to why he is so reluctant to co-operate, and draw its own conclusions about any sums of money that may be stashed away in foreign bank accounts.

Will I automatically get half my husband's pension?

Not automatically, no. The laws on pensions have changed in the last couple of years and now apply to any divorce where the original divorce petition was filed on or after 1 December 2000. The new rules say that, unlike in the previous law, it is now possible to split a pension fund between two people. For example, when a pension fund is valued, you or your spouse will be given a figure called the cash equivalent transfer value (or CETV), which is the total value of the pension fund at the date the valuation was made. This is the figure to look out for once you receive your pension documents. To put it simply, say that the CETV figure was £80,000, it is now possible to create two separate pensions out of that fund, with any values that you either agree to or that are decided by the court if matters go that far. So you could each walk away with a pension fund of £40,000, or you could get £20,000 and your spouse £60,000 depending on the circumstances.

It is not right, however, to assume (as many do) that you are automatically entitled to half the pension fund. How much you get – if anything – will depend on all the other circumstances in the case, such as the length of the marriage, whether you have a pension fund of your own, how much there is to split between you in total, and whether you are still young enough to build up your own pension fund before retirement. You should also note that you will be able to argue for a share of only that part of the pension that was built up during the time of the marriage; any part of the pension fund that your husband built up prior to your marriage will not be available to you to split in any event.

If my husband has been violent to me, will he still have the right to see the children?

In a case like this, if you are not willing to allow your ex to have contact with the children, he can apply to the courts for what is known as a Contact Order. This is an order made by a judge granting your ex the right to see the children at certain times. Before an order is made, a family court adviser will be appointed to make a recommendation as to what should happen. If the judge feels there *should* be contact, he can order that any contact should be supervised in appropriate cases (see Chapter 8).

In some cases the court decides that if domestic violence is proved (and especially where the children have witnessed it or the mother is very traumatised), it would be better for there to be no contact between the father and the children. The courts can also order that there should be 'indirect contact', which is when a parent does not actually see the children face to face but sends letters and cards instead. In other cases, contact can either be supervised or, if the family court adviser and the judge think that there is no longer a risk of violence, unsupervised. It will all depend on what the judge thinks is in the best interests of the child, given the history of the case.

If I get divorced how will I support myself?

In some cases, especially where one partner has earned a lot more money that the other, you might find that you are entitled to 'periodical payments' or, as you probably know it better, 'maintenance'. Nowadays, though, the courts try to achieve a 'clean break' (where neither person has any further connections or obligations to the other person) as often as possible, so they are no longer as keen to make maintenance orders that would last for the rest of your lives. Unless you are either near retirement age or in very poor health, if you *do* get maintenance it is likely to be for a fixed period only, enough time for you to get back on your feet again, either by retraining or waiting until the children no longer need you at home full-time. At some point you will be expected to rebuild your own life and, though the courts will consider giving you some time to do that, eventually you will be expected to start providing for yourself again without any assistance from your ex-spouse.

The other thing to remember when thinking about maintenance is that any maintenance order will come to an end if you either remarry or live with another partner for at least six months.

If I give my wife a bigger portion of the assets now, does that guarantee that the Child Support Agency will leave me alone?

No. Until 1993 it was primarily the courts that decided the level of child maintenance, but these matters are now dealt with by the Child Support Agency (CSA). Regardless of how much capital you give your spouse at the time of the divorce, as long as you are the natural parent of a child under the age of 16 (or 19 if he or she is in full-time education) then your ex can make a claim to the Child Support Agency at any time.

How much will I have to pay if my ex applies to the Child Support Agency in respect of our children?

New rules relating to maintenance calculated by the CSA have come into force very recently. Under the new system the important thing to know is that the whole process of calculating how much you should either pay (or receive) under the CSA has now become much simpler. In broad terms, absent parents are now expected to pay 15 per cent of net income for the first child, 20 per cent if there are two children and 25 per cent if there are three or more. Unlike the old system, 'net income' simply means the amount you receive once your tax has been paid, and no allowances will be made for other things such as housing costs, etc.

If my ex-wife remarries, does that mean she cannot claim from me through the CSA any more?

No, it doesn't. Any liabilities you have to your ex-wife in terms of maintenance for her are likely to stop if she remarries, but the situation is different with regard to the children. Your ex can apply to the CSA at any time, whether she has remarried or not. In the eyes of the law the absent father (or mother) of the children remains someone who has responsibility for the children whether or not the other parent is living with or married to somebody else. This means that you can be held liable for payments through the CSA at any time until the children reach the age of 16 (or 19 if in full-time education).

Does a common law wife have the same rights over me as if we had been married?

No. Although people frequently use the expression 'common law wife' there isn't really any such thing. For some reason it seems to be the general feeling that after you have lived with someone for six months you suddenly get all sorts of rights; some people even think they can get 'half of everything' after six months. This is simply nonsense. Unless you have been married, then your property will be yours if it is in your name and his if it is in his name. You do not suddenly acquire rights to your partner's property just by living with him for a short time.

If you have bought things (such as a house) together and you are not married, then you should be able to get a share of the value either by showing that you own half of it, or that you have made significant contributions to it. The fact remains, however, that you have no rights in your partner's property other than if you have contributed to it yourself, so the situation is completely different from one in which you have been married, and you should not confuse the two. Married people, rightly or wrongly, have a lot more rights (and responsibilities) than those who have simply lived together.

CHAPTER 3

CHOOSING AND MEETING A SOLICITOR

Many of the people that we meet tell us that they put off their first visit to a solicitor for many months, sometimes even years. Often by the time our clients walk through the door of the solicitor's office for the first time they have reached complete desperation, sometimes even a state of panic. The main reason for this seems to be that admitting any marriage is over is a very difficult thing to do, and seeing a solicitor seems to many people to be a very final step. It might be the first time you have been able to admit to someone else that your marriage is in serious difficulty but, while that can be tough, speaking to a solicitor about it is not a final step at all. You do not need to make any final decisions at your first meeting. In fact, if you seem to be rushing into a course of action your solicitor may well tell you to go away and think about things a bit more.

Often the first meeting can be used just to get some advice as to what you should do next or how best to deal with a particular situation. It might help just to know what your legal options are. On the other hand, it might be your spouse that has started off the divorce proceedings, and you might need to ask a solicitor how you should respond. Either way, meeting a good solicitor can often mean that a huge weight is lifted because you should come away with a much better knowledge of exactly where you stand and what is likely to happen. Even if there are difficult decisions ahead, they will always be easier once you know what the options are.

How do I find a good solicitor?

This is not always easy. As in any profession, some lawyers are better than others, and it also helps if you can find someone with whom you can strike up a rapport quickly. But how do you go about this?

The best recommendation is a personal one, so if you know someone who has recently needed to take advice about divorce or separation then ask if they were pleased with the service they got. However, it might be that you don't know anyone in this situation or that you don't feel comfortable talking about it to anyone. If you are in this category there are a few things you can do to set you in the right direction.

First of all you want someone who has expertise in family law. More and more these days, solicitors are specialising in a particular area of law, rather than doing a bit of everything as was the case in the past. You will find the names of many firms by looking in the Yellow Pages under 'Solicitors'. The advertisements will mention which areas of law are covered by that particular firm, so look for one that specifically mentions that it practises in family law, or says something about divorce and matrimonial affairs.

Then you should check that the advertisement has a symbol on it bearing the words 'Legal Aid Franchise'. Whether or not you eventually qualify for Legal Aid is not the only point here; any firm that has been given a Legal Aid Franchise has had to go through a series of rigorous checks on its procedures and practices, and has to practise in line with guidelines that are designed to offer a better service to the client. If you see this symbol advertised you can expect a certain standard of service in all your dealings with the firm. Another symbol worth noting is the one with three figures in it and the letters SFLA underneath. This means that the firm is associated to the Solicitors' Family Law Association. Take time to read the advert carefully, as some firms choose to advertise by using the standard symbols while others explain their specialities in text.

From the firms that meet all the above requirements, go on to consider how easy the office would be to get to. If you think this advice sounds at all patronising, it is worth remembering that if things become at all complex you may need to visit the solicitors' office more than once. Is it within easy reach of your home, or would you be able to get there from your workplace? A few firms of solicitors open on a Saturday also, so it may be worth ringing to check this point if you would find an appointment in the week difficult.

Once you have picked out a couple of firms, it is worth ringing them to ask if they are prepared to give you a free initial appointment. This is a very useful opportunity for you to meet the solicitor and to see what your first impression is without any obligation to you. No pressure should be put on you at this meeting; you should be able to explain briefly what the problem is and get some initial advice about where to go from there.

It is impossible to go through all the scenarios that a solicitor and client might discuss at this first meeting as every situation is so different, but you should give your solicitor as much detail as you can about your circumstances, and be prepared to answer all of their questions. Some clients need urgent help in a situation of domestic violence; some are thinking about divorce for the very first time; some have already separated and are concerned about how to arrange contact with the children; some are worried about money issues; and others may have just found out that their spouse has been having an affair and don't know where to turn next. Whatever your individual concern, try not to feel embarrassed or awkward about telling the solicitor what the problem is. Family lawyers often hear harrowing and upsetting tales and we are unlikely to be shocked by anything you say. What is probably for you one of the worst situations that you have ever faced in your life will not come as any great surprise to a solicitor, and the better informed the solicitor is about your situation, the better the advice they will be able to give.

Solicitors are not counsellors

In some ways meeting a solicitor for the first time is a bit similar to a first meeting with a doctor. You will know very quickly whether or not you feel comfortable with that person, and this is important as you will have to talk to him or her about very personal issues and feelings within a short space of time. What you must not expect is to receive counselling from your solicitor. It will come as no surprise to hear that many of our clients come for legal help when they are going through an extremely traumatic time. They often feel upset, confused and unsure about what to do next. Many are not even sure whether a divorce is what they want at all. It may be that the marriage is simply going through a rough patch.

Talking about these issues with someone you can trust is almost always helpful, even if it is just to get your own thoughts straight in your mind, but you will be disappointed if you come to a solicitor expecting him or her to fulfil the role of a counsellor. This doesn't mean that every solicitor will be unsympathetic and cold-hearted when they are listening to you; some are quite the opposite, but they will push you to concentrate on the issues that they might be able to help with. The first half hour appointment goes quickly, so if they do not seem interested in hearing every small detail of how the marriage broke down it is probably only because there are more relevant matters to be dealt with first.

Would I find counselling helpful?

A good solicitor should be able to give you some reassurance about your situation, as well as information as to your legal position, and this in itself often helps people feel better about things immediately. You will see from the stories at the end of the book that feeling more confident after the first visit to a solicitor is quite a common experience (and no – they weren't our own clients!), but there may be many other things going on in your life that will need to be resolved. A solicitor will not have the time or the expertise to deal with all of these.

Don't underestimate the help that a counsellor can give. A counsellor does a very different job to that of a solicitor, but they can be extremely helpful in allowing you not only to talk about your problems, but also to sort out what it is you are feeling and what steps you could take to improve the situation. If this passage has come across as unsympathetic and unfeeling then we promise you that is not the intention. Both writers of this book have been through a divorce and know first-hand how upsetting and traumatic it can be. There will be a whole host of issues that you will need to sort out, but it is worth thinking about who is the best person to help with those things. Although some people are still sceptical about counselling and what it can do we know of many clients who have found it an extremely useful aid in helping to get through a difficult time.

What can I expect my solicitor to do?

If you feel that your first meeting with your solicitor has been helpful, and that he or she is someone you could see yourself working with, then it is likely that you will agree either what further steps should be taken, or to come back for a further appointment. Any further action that you agree should be put in writing to you so that you know exactly what you can expect to happen next. From that point on, as your case proceeds, your solicitor will be responsible for writing letters on your behalf, filing any necessary documents at court and keeping in contact with your ex's solicitors about how the case is developing. They will also negotiate on your behalf if this becomes necessary at a later stage, and may represent you at court should matters proceed that far.

How often should I contact my solicitor?

Going through a divorce is likely to be the most important and often the most worrying thing on a person's mind. It is understandable that they will want advice and reassurance on a regular basis from the person who is supposed to be representing them. However, it is worth remembering that most solicitors are involved in many different cases at any one time, so may not always be available to take your call. It can also be difficult from a solicitor's point of view to receive a phone call and be expected to remember all the details of that case at the drop of a hat. The best thing you can do is to try and provide your solicitor with any information they have requested as soon as you are able, and if they are not available in person it is worth leaving a message with their secretary.

If you do need to speak to your solicitor in person then it is usually worth waiting until he is able to return your call, rather than ringing in repeatedly, as this way you can be more confident that he has refreshed his memory about the case prior to ringing you. You will also make yourself immensely unpopular if you become one of those clients who rings in constantly; every firm has at least one of them, and solicitors can become extremely clever at avoiding calls if someone becomes too much of a nuisance! Make sure, though, that you keep your solicitor informed if anything important does happen in the case, as they will only be able to advise you if they know what is going on, and it may take some time for them to hear it from the other side. Similarly, if any offers are made or problems raised by your ex's solicitors, then you should be told about them promptly, and you will be entitled to ask why if this doesn't happen.

When do I need a barrister?

People are still confused about the difference between solicitors and barristers. Both are lawyers, but the first contact you have with a legal adviser will always be with a solicitor. You cannot approach a barrister direct. One old way of explaining the difference between the two has been to use the example of the GP and the consultant. With any medical problem you would see your GP first, and he or she might then refer you to a consultant for more specialist advice if it was needed. In a way this is similar to the way solicitors and barristers operate, but this particular way of explaining the relationship between the two is now a little outdated. Nowadays more and more solicitors are specialising themselves, and you will find that many solicitors are experts in family law as they practise in nothing else. The reason these days for using a barrister is not so much that a solicitor needs specialist advice; it is more often when a second opinion is needed or where the matter cannot be resolved by solicitors alone and is likely to end up in court.

An example is where you have discussed with your solicitor the likely outcome in relation to your finances. As in most situations, it is very difficult to predict exactly what the outcome would be if the matter went as far as court. The solicitor will give you his or her initial opinion, and might then send the papers to a barrister to see if the barrister agrees with this opinion or has any other suggestions to put forward. Sometimes the barrister will simply look at the papers and send a written opinion or 'advice' as to what he or she thinks of the case, and in other cases the barrister may wish to meet with you to discuss matters in more detail. A meeting like this with a barrister is called a 'con' – short for 'conference'. Why we do not simply refer to meetings as meetings we do not know, but if you overhear a solicitor arranging a 'con with counsel', then at least you know what they are doing – arranging a meeting with a barrister.

If it is at all possible to resolve your particular problem without the need for going to court, then your solicitor will be able to enter into the negotiations with your ex's solicitor and draw up all the necessary paperwork, with or without a second opinion from a barrister. Sometimes, though, the two sides simply can't agree on certain matters, perhaps where the children should live, how often one parent should have contact with them, or how the assets should be split. In these situations it might be necessary for a court to decide what the outcome should be. Although solicitors are able to do many court hearings themselves nowadays, they certainly can't do all of them because of the need to stay in the office and see clients on a daily basis.

Once you are certain that a matter is going to proceed to court and that a barrister is required, a solicitor will make copies of all the relevant papers in your case, and write 'instructions to counsel', otherwise known as the 'brief'. Good instructions include a brief history of the case (which the solicitor will have gathered together from all your meetings with him), a summary of the issues to be resolved, the strengths and weaknesses of the case if this is relevant, and sometimes the solicitor's view as to the likely way forward.

You will be unlikely to have much information on how to find a good barrister. You will not find them listed in the phone book, and the likelihood is that in a straightforward case you will not need one anyway. But if you do, your solicitor will be used to dealing with certain people who also have a special interest in family law, and he or she will try and book one who is available on the court dates relevant to your case. A good solicitor will also draw on his knowledge of the barristers he has used in the past to choose one likely to strike up a working relationship with you in a short space of time.

From this point on until the end of the court process, the barrister and solicitor will keep in touch with each other about any new developments in the case, or offers of settlement from the other side. If there is anything you feel that your legal advisers should know, then the person to contact is your solicitor. The solicitor will be the person who has all your papers and your file to hand so can make a record of any progress in the case, whereas the barrister is likely to be spending most days at court on different matters. It would also become confusing if you were contacting two people about your case at different times, so keeping the solicitor informed will mean that anything important is passed on to the barrister in good time for the court hearing.

How much will all this legal work cost?

This is one of the most important questions for many people who come to see a solicitor for the first time. The amount that you pay in legal fees can vary enormously, from a few hundred pounds to several thousands. It will depend on whether you simply require a straightforward, unopposed divorce, or more complicated work to sort out issues over children or the assets. It will also depend on the individual firm, the area of the country to some extent, and whether or not the case eventually ends up in court or not. Whatever your situation, it is always worth asking the solicitor for the firm's hourly rates and an estimate of the likely costs. Do not hesitate to ask this question again as the case proceeds, as the last thing you want is to be faced with an enormous bill at the end that you simply weren't expecting. Remember that the costs will always rise dramatically if the case has to go to court, so it is worth bearing this in mind if there is a possible compromise available that would avoid having to do this.

Do I qualify for Legal Aid?

There are basically two types of Legal Aid – one is Legal Help and Help at Court, the other is Full Legal Aid.

Legal Help and Help at Court

This covers initial advice and divorce proceedings, but does not extend to representation at court except in very limited circumstances. In order to qualify for this type of help you have to be eligible on financial grounds. If you already receive Income Support or Jobseeker's Allowance then you will qualify automatically.

The exact rules on the allowable income levels change regularly so we do not want to mislead you by putting in too many exact figures that may be out of date by the time this book is published. However, to give you some idea of the amount of income that is allowed, the test at the beginning of 2003 was that your gross income could not exceed £2250 per month, and your disposable income could not be more than £611 per month. Your disposable income is worked out by taking your gross income, then deducting set allowances for each child if you have them, a set allowance if you work, and mortgage or rent repayments (capped at £545 per month). Deductions can also be made for tax, childminding, National Insurance, maintenance payments and housing costs. Even if your disposable income is below £611 per month, you could be disqualified for having too much capital, and you should check the current maximum amount of capital that is allowed with your solicitor to see whether you still qualify for Legal Aid at this level. At the time of writing it is £3000.

Full Legal Aid

This is what you will need if your case goes as far as court, e.g. if the divorce is defended, if there is a disagreement over the residence or contact of the children, or because of a contested financial case. The eligibility test for this second type of Legal Aid is the same as for Legal Help and Help at Court, except that the minimum figure of disposable income that you are allowed to have is currently £695, with a capital limit of £8000. The exception to this capital rule comes in a contested case over the financial side of a divorce. Here, even if there is capital available, until a final order has been made as to how the assets should be split between the parties (even if you have agreed the outcome between yourselves), this capital is known as 'capital in dispute' and will not count against you in terms of your eligibility for Legal Aid.

Unfortunately, for either type of Legal Aid the Legal Services Commission does not take into account any payments you have to make for loans, credit cards, utility bills or other indebtedness.

If you are in any doubt as to whether you might qualify for Legal Aid, make sure you ask your solicitor to assess your financial position. Also remember that, if you think you do qualify for Legal Aid, you must approach a firm with a Legal Aid Franchise as only these firms will be able to take on Legal Aid work. Legal Aid Franchise symbols often appear on a firm's letterhead and in its phone book entry, but if you are still not sure whether the firm is allowed to take on this type of work you should ask. If you are told that the firm you have approached only does private work, then it is worth making absolutely sure that you would not qualify for Legal Aid before you start down the road of paying private fees. The service you receive as a private client is unlikely to be any better, but you will soon see the difference when the bill arrives!

CHAPTER 4

THE GROUNDS FOR GETTING A DIVORCE

In writing this book we asked many solicitors for their views as to the most common myths and misunderstandings that people have about divorce. One of the ones that came up most often was that many people still think you can get divorced simply by saying that the marriage has 'broken down irretrievably'. In some ways this would be a good idea; it would mean that any two people who thought their marriage was no longer worth continuing could go ahead and make that decision in a nice civilised way without having to blame either person. Unfortunately, this get-out clause from your marriage vows, though potentially useful, does not exist.

You cannot get a divorce either because you have 'grown apart', have 'become bored' or are 'no longer compatible'. To divorce within England and Wales you need to prove one of four things:

- That your spouse has committed adultery and that you can no longer tolerate living with him/her.

- That your spouse has behaved in such a manner that you cannot reasonably be expected to live with him/her. This is also commonly referred to, though not strictly accurately, as 'unreasonable behaviour'.

- That you have been separated from your spouse for at least two years and you both consent to the divorce OR that you have been separated from your spouse for at least five years if your spouse will not give consent to the divorce.

- That you have been 'deserted' by your spouse for a period of not less than two years.

Still confused? We will try and explain each of the above in simple terms, but the first point to note is that the law says that you cannot get divorced within the first year of marriage. There are still many people who are not aware of this being the case, and it can come as a shock to those who realise that their marriage will not stand the test of time after just a few short weeks or months. Nevertheless, that is what the law says, so even if you know your marriage is over soon after it started, you will have to wait at least 12 months before you can issue a divorce petition.

ADULTERY

Can I get divorced because I have been unfaithful myself?

No, you cannot. Clients often come to us thinking that because they have had an affair while still being married, this entitles them to seek a divorce from their spouse. This is not true. In order to divorce someone on the grounds of adultery, you have to be able to show that your spouse has committed adultery against you. If this is the ground you choose on which to divorce your husband or wife, it is worth remembering that it is up to you to prove to the court that he/she has been unfaithful. Legally, the term adultery means that your spouse has had sexual intercourse with another person during the time that you were married; any type of affair or sexual conduct that does not involve intercourse itself would not be enough to satisfy the label of adultery for the purposes of divorce.

How do I prove it?

The most common way to satisfy a court that adultery has happened, believe it or not, is for the adulterer to admit it. This does not happen (at least not usually) by him giving live evidence to the court, but simply by him ticking a box on a form. When you first file for divorce (see Chapter 5, pages 55–56) you will be asked on the form to state the reason you believe a divorce is justified. If you have said that the ground is adultery, then your spouse will know this when he receives the paperwork (or Acknowledgement of Service) (see page 56). There is a box on this form asking whether or not he has committed adultery, and if the answer is yes, then this admission is enough to show the court that the adultery has occurred.

Do I have to know the name of the person he committed adultery with?

No. It is enough that you can show to the court that the adultery has happened; you do not need to know the name of the person it happened with. If you do know the person's name, you are entitled to name them on the divorce petition if you wish to do so. This person then becomes what is known as a 'co-respondent', and can choose to take part in the divorce proceedings (at least in relation to the adultery allegations) if they want to.

What if he does not tick the box admitting to adultery?

If your spouse does not wish to admit the adultery then it will be up to you to prove to the court that it has happened. You would have to have some sort of evidence that a sexual relationship has existed between your spouse and someone else. If you come up against this situation you will have to think back to the ways in which you first found out about it yourself. Did someone tell you? Did you find evidence of an affair? It may be that the evidence that would prove the adultery is already there. If not, and the adultery is still continuing, some clients go down the route of hiring a private detective who will find the evidence for them. In reality though, if your spouse simply won't admit that he has been unfaithful to you, it may be easier to pursue the divorce on grounds of unreasonable behaviour, which we shall cover next.

Although you may wonder why this is necessary, the law as it stands requires that you show, in addition to the adultery itself, that it is 'intolerable for you to live with the Respondent' (i.e. your spouse).

Generally, you will not be asked to do anything more than show to the court that the adultery has happened, but you will see when your solicitor fills in the papers that it says: 'The Respondent has committed adultery and the Petitioner finds it intolerable to live with the Respondent.' It is drafted in this way because this is what the law still demands. The 'intolerable' part of the adultery ground becomes relevant when thinking about one further point:

If you live with your spouse for six months after finding about the adultery then this ground for divorce is void.

Current law says that you will lose your right to divorce using the ground of adultery if you have lived together with your spouse for six months or more *after you found out about the adultery*. I have emphasised those words, because it does not matter if the adultery itself happened some time ago; your six months starts running from the day that you found out about it. This may seem strange, but the law seems to be saying that if you know your spouse has been unfaithful, and you can manage to live with that fact (and him) for six months, then it would appear that it cannot be intolerable for you to live with him, so the second part of the test has not been met. If, however, you find out about the adultery, try to get back together with your spouse, and things do not work out between you, then you will not be barred from relying on the adultery as a ground for divorce as long as your time back together with your spouse does not add up to more than six months.

The one saving grace in this part of the law is that if you at some later stage find out about another act of adultery (whether it is with the same person or with someone else) then your time period starts again and, as long as you do not spend a further six months living with your spouse, you will still be entitled to file for divorce on the grounds of adultery. Also, there is no time limit for citing adultery as an example of unreasonable behaviour.

UNREASONABLE BEHAVIOUR

It is a joke among divorce lawyers that any half-decent solicitor can find unreasonable behaviour in any marriage if they look for it hard enough. There may be some truth in that. There can't be very many of us who have been married who can honestly say that they have never behaved unreasonably! Most of us do it far too often.

To get divorced on the grounds of 'unreasonable behaviour' (that is the way most people describe it, including lawyers, even though it is not strictly accurate) you have to show the following: that your spouse has behaved in such a way that you can no longer reasonably be expected to live with him.

What sort of things would my spouse have to do for me to divorce him on these grounds?

It would be possible to write an entire book on this subject. People find all sorts of behaviour impossible to live with, and to a large extent that depends on the type of person that you are, and the beliefs and values that you as an individual have. Domestic violence is often given as the type of behaviour that you cannot be expected to live with, but emotional abuse can be just as damaging. Constant name-calling or put-downs can often be one of the reasons given for divorcing under this heading. I have seen divorce petitions where it was claimed a husband groped another woman's breasts in public, another where the wife could no longer stand to live with her husband's obsession with pornography, and several based on a spouse having a gambling addiction, a drink problem or even suffering from long-term and severe depression. Many divorce petitions base unreasonable behaviour on something to do with the sexual relationship, e.g. your spouse refuses any type of sexual contact, or he makes demands of you that you simply cannot abide.

There are many different ways of drafting the papers when the divorce is based on your spouse's behaviour, and when your solicitor shows you the document you must say if you are not happy with any part of it. You must remember that that document will be seen by your spouse once it has been sent to him by the court, and you need to think about the way he is likely to react to it, especially if you are still in contact with each other or, as in some cases, still living together.

You can be almost certain that when your spouse comes to read the document, it will not make comfortable reading. It is not just the fact that he will see a list of his faults down on paper, he will also know that his other half has been discussing the intimate details of his marriage with a solicitor, who is paid to be on her side, and who will have taken most of what has been said at face value. You may ask yourself why this should matter if you are getting divorced anyway, but it is a point worth giving serious thought to. Do you have children together? Will you still have to see each other because of the children having contact? Are you still arguing over finances? Will you have to come into contact in some other way, perhaps through work or through friends?

A divorce is never easy, but the way a divorce is conducted can have a long-lasting impact on both you and the manner of future communication with your ex, even if this is something you would rather never have to do. There are certain things in life that people never forget, prime examples being births, deaths, marriages and divorces. So, however angry, bitter, hurt and depressed you may be feeling, it is worth giving careful thought to how your divorce petition is worded.

It is inevitable of course that you will have to blame your spouse for his conduct. That is what the law asks you to do. You have to show, by way of examples, that he has behaved in a way that you cannot live with. Of course you are going to have to say some negative things, but how much detail do you want to give? Do you wish to petition for divorce all guns blazing, highlighting all the things that have hurt you and all the ways in which he has behaved wrongly? Or would it be safer to ask your solicitor to frame the document in such a way that you can show unreasonable behaviour without obviously trying to humiliate your spouse?

In writing the above we do not try and persuade you either way. Everybody going through a divorce feels differently about the process. Some are sad, others relieved; some want it over as quickly and painlessly as possible, others want their ex to suffer as much as possible. Only you will know what it is you are feeling. Just remember that the hurdle of showing unreasonable behaviour can be met in many different ways, and it is worth spending a little time considering how it might be best to do it in your particular case.

What happens if my spouse won't admit to the behaviour I accuse him of?

In Chapter 5 we cover more fully all the steps involved in the divorce process and also what happens if your spouse chooses to defend the divorce, but it *is* possible for the divorce to proceed without your spouse actually making any admissions as to his behaviour. We should also point out that for a divorce to actually go as far as to be defended in court is extremely rare.

Many people are upset when they read what has been written about them and wish to spend a large amount of time explaining how none of it is true. On the other hand, however upset the person is about what is alleged, they are often prepared to admit that the marriage is over, whatever the grounds. For example, a husband accused of unreasonable behaviour might be completely adamant that none of the allegations is true. At the same time, though, he might agree that divorce is the only way forward and there is no way that the marriage can be saved. In a situation like this, rather than going to the lengths of denying all the allegations and then for the husband to issue his own proceedings detailing the wife's unreasonable behaviour against *him*, the easiest solution in some cases is for the husband to agree 'not to defend the divorce without admitting any of the allegations made against him'.

In plain English this simply means that he allows the divorce to go ahead, he admits in principle that he has behaved in such a way that his wife cannot be expected to live with him, but he does not admit any of the individual things that she might have accused him of doing. This can be a way of allowing the divorce to go ahead without going to all the trouble and expense of denying everything and starting again from scratch.

SEPARATION

The third way that a divorce can be obtained in this country is through separation. If you and your spouse have been separated for two years or more, and you both agree to the divorce going ahead, then this is a ground for divorce. This is the quickest time that you will be able to divorce without any allegations of blame being made about your former spouse.

What does separation actually mean?

Separation as far as divorce law is concerned means living as two separate households. Most often this happens when a couple physically split up from each other, and one leaves the home that they have been living in together. However, it is also possible to be separated while still living under the same roof. To show this, it is not enough just to claim that things have been rocky for a couple of years in the marriage. You must show that you have actually been living as separate households, so that you no longer share a bed, you do not choose to spend vast amounts of your leisure time together, and you do not arrange your finances or household duties as a normal couple would be likely to do.

As with the six month rule relating to adultery, any period of time of six months or more that you have lived together again as husband and wife will start the clock ticking again. So, for example, you separate for two years, then get back together for eight months, realise that it has not worked, and then go back to relying on the two years that you were apart in applying for the divorce. In the court's view, the fact that you have been reconciled for that eight-month period cancels out the previous two-year separation as a ground for getting divorced.

The two year separation rule is a fairly common way of getting divorced, and the advantage of it is clearly that no one has to take the blame for any conduct, be it adultery or unreasonable behaviour. It is enough that both people agree that, following two years apart, the divorce should go ahead.

What happens if my spouse will not agree to divorce me after two years' separation?

If this is the situation you are in then, unless you can go back to one of the other grounds for divorce listed above, your only choice is to wait for a further three years, until a total of five years has passed with you living separately, at which point your spouse's consent is no longer needed. After this length of time, as long as you can show that your separation has been for five years or more, and that you have not lived together for any period or periods totalling more than six months during that time, then you will be entitled to a divorce whether your spouse consents or not.

DESERTION

To use desertion as a ground for divorce nowadays is extremely rare. It is much more likely that you will be able to use one of the other grounds. However, just for the sake of completeness, in order to prove desertion you must show that your spouse has left you, with the intention that your co-habitation should be permanently at an end, and this must have been for a minimum period of two years. So if, for example, your husband decides to work abroad for a period, but still considers himself to be married to you, then this is not desertion in the legal sense. It is also essential that to prove desertion you are not in fact living with each other any more. This is different to separation, where it is possible to argue that you have been separated even while still living under the same roof.

If you decided to argue that you had been deserted, you would also have to show that when your spouse deserted you this was not as a result of mutual decision, but that he walked out on you without your consent. As already stated, it is extremely unusual to use desertion as a ground for getting divorced, as you are far more likely to be able to prove one of the other, more common, grounds in your petition.

Why should we have to have grounds in the first place? If the marriage isn't working, isn't that a good enough reason in itself?

There are many people who think that two people who have chosen to marry should have the right in law to terminate that marriage at any time, and without having to give any reason other than that they simply do not want it to continue. It is argued that if two people agree that a marriage is over, then that should be a good enough reason for ending it in itself. On the other hand opponents of this view say that to introduce laws of this kind would undermine the whole meaning of marriage and would make marriage vows, and the institution of marriage itself, meaningless. Whatever your personal view on how a marriage should have to come to an end in legal terms, the law as it stands still only allows divorces to proceed on the specific grounds that are listed above.

It may be that this is something that will change in the future but, until it does, it is worth taking some time, if you are thinking about a divorce, to consider what the grounds for that divorce are likely to be in your case, and whether you think you will be able to satisfy the court that these grounds exist. Your solicitor will be able to give you advice as to the best way to proceed once you have explained your situation to her.

---CHAPTER 5---

A STEP-BY-STEP GUIDE TO THE DIVORCE PROCESS

This chapter will attempt to explain to you all the various stages involved in getting a divorce, from the initial divorce petition right through to when the divorce is finalised, known as the decree absolute. To begin with we will explain the procedure when your spouse allows the divorce to go ahead without 'defending' it. What happens when your spouse either defends the divorce or refuses to co-operate is explained further on in the chapter.

We should also mention that it is possible to get divorced without having to use the services of a solicitor at all. In this case, the procedure for getting divorced would essentially be the same as in this chapter. However, 'do-it-yourself' divorces are still relatively unusual, and this book has not been written with that market in mind as it goes on to deal with issues of the finances and the children, which generally do require the assistance of a solicitor at some stage.

If you are certain that you want to divorce and you do not wish to use the services of a solicitor, there are leaflets available at your local county court that will guide you through the process, and there are also books that deal specifically with this subject. In this chapter and elsewhere in the book, we have assumed that in getting divorced you have chosen to do this with the help of a solicitor.

In summary the stages involved in a divorce are:

1. Meeting a solicitor

2. Preparing and filing the divorce petition (and the Statement of Arrangements if there are children)

3. The Notice of Proceedings is sent to the Respondent by the court, together with a copy of the Petition (and the Statement of Arrangements if there are children)

4. The Acknowledgement of Service is returned by the Respondent to the court

5. The courts grants a Certificate of Entitlement to a decree

6. The decree nisi is granted by the court

7. The decree absolute is granted by the court

We have used the legal terms that lawyers use to describe the various stages of a divorce. You will no doubt hear these expressions throughout the divorce proceedings so it is as well to know what they all mean. We will explain each of the above in turn.

1. Meeting a solicitor

By now you should have read pages 33–37 of Chapter 3, which cover your first meeting with a solicitor. As we explained earlier, it may well be that at this first meeting you have not yet made a firm decision about issuing divorce proceedings. Many clients first come to the office because they are hurt or upset about their spouse's behaviour, or because they have just found out about an affair and feel upset, humiliated and angry. However, these things do not necessarily mean that the marriage is over, and it is quite common for clients to come in talking about the possibility of a divorce without being at all sure that they in fact want one. We must stress that there is nothing wrong with this at all. Solicitors do not exist to break up marriages, and if a marriage going through a difficult time can be saved then so much the better. However, there may come a time when you have reached a firm decision to get divorced. Once this decision has been made, you will go on to decide together with your solicitor which grounds for divorce best apply in your particular circumstances (see Chapter 4). Your solicitor will then draw up a document known as the 'divorce petition'.

2. Preparing the divorce petition

The divorce petition is a document giving details of the date of your marriage, whether there are any children, the reasons you are seeking a divorce and any other orders in relation to the divorce that you would like the court to make. I have included an example of a straightforward divorce petition at the end of this chapter.

If you are the person starting off the divorce process, and instructing your solicitor to prepare the petition for you, then you become known as the 'Petitioner'. The petition must make clear the grounds for divorce that you are relying on. The possible grounds for divorce are adultery, your spouse behaving in such a way that you can no longer live with him ('unreasonable behaviour'), desertion, separation for two years (where both consent to the divorce) OR separation for five years (see Chapter 4). You will also need to provide your original marriage certificate or a certified copy.

Statement of Arrangements for the Children

If you have children, your solicitor will also have to prepare this document. It asks questions about the names and ages of the children, plans for their schooling, any health concerns, where the children are going to live, plans for contact with the absent parent etc. The issues dealt with by the Statement of Arrangements are covered more fully in Chapter 8.

These documents are then filed at the county court (either you yourself or the solicitor can do this), together with a copy of your marriage certificate and a fee. You will need three copies of these documents: one copy is kept by you and two are sent to the court, which will keep one and send the other copy to your spouse. If your ground for divorce is adultery and you are naming a co-respondent, you will need a fourth copy of the petition for that person; the court will ensure that the co-respondent receives this copy and an Acknowledgement of Service.

Once these documents have been filed with the court, your solicitor will receive a form called the 'notice of issue of petition'. This will give you a number for the divorce proceedings and tell you when the documents are sent to your spouse.

3. Notice of Proceedings to the Respondent

Once the above documents have been filed with the court, copies of them are sent by the court directly to your spouse, who becomes known as the 'Respondent'. As well as the copy of the divorce petition you have filed with the court (and a copy of the Statement of Arrangements for the Children if this applies to you), your spouse will receive another document which is called the 'Acknowledgement of Service'.

4. The Acknowledgement of Service

Once the Respondent has received the documents, he has eight days in which to return the Acknowledgement of Service to the court. Its return tells the court two important things. First, it reassures the court that the Respondent has in fact received the papers and knows that there is a divorce underway. A court could not consider granting a divorce unless it was sure that the Respondent either knew about the proceedings, or was deliberately avoiding receiving the documents from the court. The second purpose that the Acknowledgement of Service serves is that it asks the Respondent to say something about whether he intends to allow the divorce to proceed or whether he opposes it. The Respondent must also comment on the proposals you have made in the Statement of Arrangements for the Children, if this applies to you. Once the Court has received the Acknowledgement of Service back from the Respondent, your solicitor will receive a copy of it from the court, who will in turn contact you.

The Special Procedure List

One of the questions that the Respondent is asked on the Acknowledgement of Service is whether or not he intends to defend the divorce. (In plain English this means he is asked whether or not he agrees that the divorce can go ahead on the grounds that you have put down in the divorce petition: if he is not willing for it to go ahead, this is called 'defending' the divorce).

If he *does* agree to it going ahead (i.e. he is not defending the divorce), your solicitor can apply to the court for 'directions for trial'. This is done by filling in two forms that state the grounds you are relying on for the divorce and confirm what you put in the original divorce petition. They also state that your spouse is not planning to defend the divorce. Even if your solicitor fills these forms in for you, you must sign them and swear them to be true in front of a witness (either your solicitor or an officer of the court). Once these forms are returned to the court, this is known as 'entering your case in the Special Procedure List', and the papers in the case will then be put before a judge. In a divorce that is not defended by the Respondent, you will not have to attend court.

5/6. Certificate of Entitlement to a decree and the decree nisi

Once all the relevant documents have been returned to the court, a district judge will consider them without either you or your spouse having to be present. The judge will look first at the papers filed by the Petitioner that set out the grounds for divorce. If she is satisfied that the grounds have been met, and that your spouse is not defending the divorce, then you will be granted a document called a 'Certificate of Entitlement to a decree'. This document tells you the time and date when the judge will grant the first stage of the divorce, or the decree nisi. You do not have to attend on this date either. This is the first stage of the divorce completed. (An example of a decree nisi is shown at the end of this chapter, page 65.)

What happens with the Statement of Arrangements for the Children?

The judge will consider the Statement of Arrangements for the Children and the answers that the Respondent has filed to it at the same time that the decree nisi is considered. If the judge is satisfied with the arrangements, you will receive a certificate stating this and the divorce will proceed. If the judge is *not* satisfied with the proposed arrangements for any reason then you will be told this. A judge can then either request further information, ask you and the Respondent to come and see him at court, or ask for a family court adviser to prepare a report on the situation. In rare circumstances a judge can decide that you will not receive the decree absolute until you have reached satisfactory arrangements in relation to the children (see Chapter 8).

7. The court grants the decree absolute

Once you have received the decree nisi, you can then go about applying for the decree absolute, which is the final stage of the divorce process. You must wait for six weeks and one day following the date of the decree nisi before you can apply for the absolute, but the application for the absolute itself is very straightforward, and is generally granted without delay. Your solicitor will fill in the necessary form and file it with the court.

If you are the Respondent in divorce proceedings, and the Petitioner (who started the whole process off) for some reason does not go ahead and apply for the decree absolute, then you can take this matter into your own hands, as long as you wait first for the period of six weeks and a day to pass, and then for a further three months to elapse.

Once the decree absolute is granted, the divorce is over and the marriage is at an end. You are free to remarry once (and not before) the court has granted the decree absolute.

QUESTIONS ON THE DIVORCE PROCESS

Can anyone divorce in England and Wales?

In order to divorce in England and Wales, one or both of you must have your permanent homes or be living in England or Wales when the divorce petition is started. In legal terms, this is described as being either 'domiciled' or 'habitually resident' in this country. Very broadly, to be domiciled somewhere means that that place is your permanent home, and to be described as being 'habitually resident' in England or Wales you must have lived in the country for at least a year by the time of the divorce petition.

What do I need to do if I am the Respondent in the divorce?

If you are the person who has received a copy of the divorce petition that your spouse has filed, then now is the time to approach a solicitor (if you have not already done so), who will help you fill in the forms and advise you as to what to do next. You will need to make sure that you return any documents that you receive promptly to the court. If you are not happy for the divorce to go ahead, or disagree with the grounds for the divorce that the Petitioner has put on the divorce petition, then you must tell your solicitor immediately so you can decide what to do about it.

What happens if the Respondent does not return the Acknowledgement of Service to the court?

The court will let you know that it has not received the Acknowledgement of Service back from the Respondent. If the only problem is that the address you had for the Respondent was wrong, then you can provide the new address and the court will send out the documents again. If you know that you have the correct address and the Respondent is just ignoring the forms, than your solicitor can ask the court to have the forms delivered to the Respondent personally by a bailiff. Once the bailiff has served the forms on the Respondent, the court will know that the Respondent has received them, even if he chooses to carry on ignoring them. This way, it is possible for a divorce to proceed even where the Respondent will not co-operate at all.

What happens if the judge thinks the grounds for a divorce have not been met?

It is unusual for a judge to refuse to grant a decree nisi but it can happen. If for any reason the judge thinks that the grounds for a divorce have not been met, or there is some other problem with the documents, then your solicitor will be told that the judge has refused to grant the Certificate of Entitlement to a decree and also the reasons that this has happened. If this occurs you will either need to provide more information to the court, or in exceptional circumstances you might have to come to a court hearing to deal with the problem that the judge has found. In either event, your solicitor will know which steps need to be taken in order to obtain the decree nisi.

What happens if the Respondent defends the divorce?

If the Respondent in a divorce case decides to defend the divorce, he will make this clear when he returns the Acknowledgement of Service to the court. He will also have to provide an 'Answer' to the petition within 29 days to say why he has chosen to defend it. This is a document that sets out all the reasons that the Respondent gives for not agreeing that the divorce should proceed. Once this happens, the Petitioner will have to prove to the court that the grounds for divorce she has put on the petition exist. If the Respondent carries on denying they are true, then in rare cases there can be a court hearing where both the Petitioner and the Respondent give evidence, and the judge decides whether the grounds have been proved or not. This is called a contested divorce. It is unusual, however, for matters to get this far.

Sometimes when a divorce is defended it is because a Respondent cannot accept the marriage is over and he does not want it to end. In these cases, what normally happens is that once the Respondent realises that the Petitioner has made up her mind that she wants the divorce to go ahead, he will eventually back down and let the divorce proceed. (If he doesn't, then there will have to be a court hearing on whether the grounds can be proved or not, as explained above.) In other cases, the Respondent agrees that there should be a divorce, but is not happy to be the one taking the blame for it. In this case, the Respondent can issue his own divorce petition (known as a 'cross-petition'). This is basically starting the divorce proceedings again, but this time the Petitioner becomes the Respondent, and is then in a position to decide whether to agree to the grounds for divorce or defend them.

Where this happens, either one party will allow the other's petition to proceed and withdraw his own, or the case can go ahead by what is known as 'cross decrees', which means that in effect both parties divorce each other.

What happens if the Respondent says he is going to defend the divorce but then doesn't provide the court with an Answer to the divorce petition within 29 days?

If the Respondent is serious about defending the divorce, he only has 29 days in which to provide the Answer as to why he is defending it to the court. If he does not do this, then the court will assume that he no longer wishes to defend the divorce, and will continue through the procedure as if he had not indicated his intention to defend the divorce in the first place.

Example Divorce Petition

IN THE ANYTOWN COUNTY COURT

No of Matter XYZ 1234ZZ

The Petition of MARY SMITH

Shows that

1. On the 17th day of November 1985 the Petitioner

MARY SMITH was lawfully married to BOB SMITH

(Hereinafter called the Respondent) at the Register Office in the District of ANYWHERE in the County of ANYCOUNTY.

(This names both husband and wife, and shows the date and place of the marriage. Remember that the Petitioner is whichever person first starts the divorce proceedings.)

2. The Petitioner and the Respondent last lived together as husband and wife at

1, High Street, ANY TOWN.

(This address is known as the former matrimonial home.)

3. The court has jurisdiction under Article 2(1) of the Council regulation on the following ground(s)

The Petitioner and Respondent are domiciled in England and Wales and always have been habitually resident in England and Wales.

(Section 3 shows that by the parties living within England and Wales the divorce can be dealt with in the English and Welsh Court system. Different laws apply in Scotland.)

4. The Petitioner is by occupation a Shop Assistant and resides at 1, High Street, ANYTOWN

The Respondent is by occupation an Accountant and resides at 34, Different Street, Closeby Town.

5. There are two children of the family now living

Anna Smith born 10th January 1997

Benjamin Smith born 11th February 1998.

---

6. No other child now living has been born to the Petitioner during the marriage.

7. There are or have been no other proceedings in any court in England and Wales with reference to the marriage (or to any children of the family) or between the Petitioner and Respondent with reference to any property of either or both or them.

(This part just shows that these are the only court proceedings that exist in relation to this marriage.)

8. There are or have been no proceedings in the Child Support Agency with reference to the maintenance of any child of the family.

9. There are no proceedings continuing in any country outside England and Wales which relate to the marriage or are capable or affecting its validity or subsistence.

(This part is just to ensure that there are no court proceedings outside the UK that could mean that the marriage was not valid.)

10.   The said marriage has broken down irretrievably.

11.   The Respondent has behaved in such a way that the Petitioner cannot reasonably be expected to live with the Respondent.

(This is the reason that the Petitioner gives, or the 'grounds' for the breakdown of this marriage. In this case the example is unreasonable behaviour, but any of the grounds listed in Chapter 4 would be inserted here.)

12.   Particulars herewith.

(This just means that further details of the unreasonable behaviour that the Petitioner complains about are attached on a separate sheet.)

Prayer

The Petitioner therefore prays

(1) That the said marriage may be dissolved

(2) That the Petitioner may be granted the following ancillary relief:-

(i)   (an order for a Maintenance Pending Suit)

(ii) (a Periodical Payments Order)

(iii) (a Secured Provision Order)

(iv) (a Lump Sum Order)

(v)   (a Property Adjustment Order)

(vi) (a Pension Sharing Order)

(The above section, all in standard legal jargon, is a summary of what the Petitioner is asking from the Court, i.e. that the marriage be ended and a divorce granted, and that orders are made in respect of the finances. There are many different types of order that can be made in relation to the finances, so the standard form includes them all. You can either cross certain ones out or leave them all in and choose at a later date which apply to you. See Chapter 7 for more details).

Signed

   MARY SMITH

The names and addresses of the person who are to be served with this

Petition are:

Respondent:

   BOB SMITH

   34, Different Street, Closeby Town.

(This Respondent is of course your spouse, although if you had named someone as being a person your spouse had committed adultery with, they too would be named as a Respondent in this section.)

The Petitioner's address for service is

   ABC Solicitors,

   High Street, ANYTOWN

(This is the address of your solicitors, and means that any correspondence from the court or from your spouse's solicitors will go direct to the firm.)

Dated this 1st day of January 2003.

Particulars of Unreasonable Behaviour

1 The Respondent has made it clear for some time that he does not wish to spend any time with the Petitioner, and leads an almost separate existence, spending the majority of his time watching the television in the spare room.

2 The Respondent has on many occasions insulted the Petitioner in public and in front of her work colleagues and friends. He has been verbally abusive towards her, regularly describing her as 'fat' and 'ugly'.

3 The Respondent has been extremely possessive towards the Petitioner whenever they have been out together, often losing his temper if she even speaks to another man. He has accused her on more than one occasion of having an affair when this allegation is completely unfounded.

4 The Respondent has always drunk alcohol, but has recently started drinking very large amounts of alcohol on a regular basis and passes out most evenings having drunk excessively for most of the evening.

5 The Respondent has, for the last six months, not allowed the Petitioner to have any access to funds in the joint account and has hidden all her cheque books and bank cards. The Petitioner has had to live on her own very limited funds which total no more than £250 per month from her part-time cleaning job.

6 The Respondent has made sexual demands of the Petitioner which the Petitioner finds degrading and humiliating. The Respondent has an almost obsessive interest in pornography which the Petitioner does not share and has regularly demanded that the Petitioner watches videos with him which she finds intolerable.

7 In all the circumstances, the Petitioner feels that the marriage has broken down irretrievably and that she can no longer tolerate living in an environment such as the one described above.

(This example of unreasonable behaviour lists many different things that the Respondent is said to have done. You could include far fewer examples of unreasonable behaviour, or more, depending on the circumstances of your case.)

Example of a Decree Nisi

In The ANYTOWN County Court

No. of matter:

BETWEEN MARY SMITH   PETITIONER

AND BOB SMITH   RESPONDENT

AND   CO-RESPONDENT

Before District Judge BLOGGS sitting at ANYTOWN County Court

On the 1st day of January 2003

The Judge held that the respondent Bob Smith

has committed adultery

and that the Petitioner finds it intolerable to live with the Respondent,

that the marriage solemnised on

at

between Mary Smith the Petitioner

and Bob Smith the Respondent

has broken down irretrievably and decreed that the said marriage be dissolved unless sufficient cause be shown to the Court **within six weeks** from the making of this decree why such decree should not be made absolute.

Notes
This is not the final decree. Application for the final decree (decree absolute) must be made to the court. *(For guidance see leaflet D187. "I have a decree-nisi what must I do next")*

CHAPTER 6

MEDIATION

Much of this book centres on the legal side of the divorce process, the relationship you will have with your solicitor and how the court system operates, but of course there are still many cases where a husband and wife are able to agree on the important issues without having to rely too heavily on the legal system to do it for them. One of the ways that you might be able to talk through areas of disagreement is by using one of the many mediation services round the country that exist for this purpose.

What is mediation?

Mediation is a service designed to help people who are either divorcing or separating come to decisions about their future arrangements. Examples of the types of issues that might be dealt with at mediation are financial or property matters, or issues to do with the children such as residence or contact. The mediation service is completely independent of the court process. It is important to remember that mediation does not exist to offer counselling, to persuade couples to get back together, or to offer legal advice. Mediators will not make decisions for you either. Mediation exists simply to provide an opportunity to see whether there is any room for compromise and agreement after both people have had a fair chance to air their views. If a mediator thinks that counselling would help in your particular case, then he or she may suggest this as a way forward for you.

How does it work?

Both you and your ex will meet with a mediator (sometimes two), who is a person with a background in either law or family work and who has received specialist training in mediation. This will happen in a private and neutral setting. A mediator will not take sides during the mediation process, but will attempt to help both people discuss the relevant issues in an impartial way and come to a decision that suits them both. They will ensure that both people have a fair chance to put their point of view across so that discussions do not become one-sided, with one or other person taking over.

At what stage should we think about using mediation?

You can approach the mediation service at any time during the divorce or separation process. It doesn't matter if you have already issued legal proceedings, as courts will allow you time to attempt an agreement through mediation wherever that might be possible.

How will I know if mediation is right for me?

Mediation does not work in every situation. It is essential that both you and your ex agree that you are willing to give mediation a try, as it would be impossible to make progress if one person is simply not prepared to even attempt it. It is also important that neither party feels threatened or dominated by the other, so in some cases where there has been recent domestic violence, it may be that mediation is not the appropriate way forward. If you are not sure whether mediation could work in your case, then you can still phone your local mediation service, and see a mediator to discuss your situation either on your own, or together with your ex-partner.

How much does mediation cost?

There is no standard fee for mediation. Mediators usually charge an hourly rate, and this is something you will be able to find out easily from your local mediation service. Many mediation services will offer a first appointment free of charge. You may be entitled to receive financial help from the Legal Services Commission (Legal Aid) to cover the costs of mediation, and some mediation services also have bursary funds, which you can apply for if you are on a low income and would otherwise find it difficult to meet the cost of mediation. What is certain, though, is that any couple who are able to agree matters through mediation rather than having to rely on the court system will save hundreds of pounds in legal costs by doing so.

How long does it take?

Every couple will have their own individual issues to deal with at mediation, but on average it is suggested that couples will need anywhere between one and six sessions in order to deal with the matters that affect them. Each session usually lasts from an hour to an hour and a half.

Do the matters we discuss in mediation remain confidential?

Yes they do. You can rest assured that any discussions you have as part of the mediation process will not be divulged to anyone unless this is something you both agree on. If you find that you are unable to reach any final decisions through mediation and end up having to go to court, then none of the discussions you have had in mediation will be used in the court proceedings. This way you can feel free to express your point of view during mediation without having to worry that it might count against you in some way at a later date. The only exception to the confidentiality rule is if issues arise during mediation that make it apparent that someone (especially a child) is at risk of significant harm. If this is the case, then the mediator will have to inform social services of this risk.

What happens if we reach agreement?

At the end of mediation, the mediator will assist the couple in preparing an agreed statement, which sets out exactly what has been agreed and any matters that might still be in dispute. You will each receive a copy of it, and a copy may also be sent to your solicitors. These statements are not legally binding, but should help your solicitors draw up a court order that represents the issues you have agreed if this is required.

How do I find out about a mediation service near me?

There are currently around 70 mediation services around the country. To find your local service, you can ask at any county court for a copy of the *Handbook of the UK College of Family Mediators*, which will contain a list of its members and their addresses. You can also ring National Family Mediation on 020 7485 8809 or 020 7485 9066 to find out the details of your local mediation service. To find a mediation service that can provide mediation through the Community Legal Service (Legal Aid), you can either check in the local *Community Legal Service Directory* (available at local libraries), look on the CLS website at www.justask.org.uk or ring the CLS helpline on 0845 6081122.

CHAPTER 7

MONEY MATTERS

One of the central issues for any couple thinking about divorce is how best to split the assets and sort out their long-term financial position. People are understandably worried about whether they will lose the house, how they will support themselves once the divorce is over, and how to decide who should get what from the marriage.

In many cases, all these issues can be sorted out without having to go to court. Sometimes a divorcing couple can come to their own agreement about how all the assets should be split, and often solicitors can help you arrive at an agreement by advising you as to what a reasonable settlement would be and then negotiating with the solicitor on the other side. If an agreement on the finances can't be reached in this way, then either the husband or the wife will have to issue an application to have all the financial matters decided in court by a judge. The court process nowadays is made up of three different stages, which are set out on pages 87–97. You may well also come to hear the term 'ancillary relief' being used. This is simply a legal term that describes the whole process of sorting out the finances at the end of a marriage through the court system.

The one problem in writing a chapter such as this is that there is no specific formula for deciding exactly how the finances should be arranged once a marriage is at an end. No book can give you an exact answer as to what will happen in any individual situation. Even if the matter gets to court, judges have a huge amount of discretion in deciding the final outcome of each case, and two judges may decide the same case in a completely different way. What we can tell you, however, is the possible financial orders that a court can make, what factors a court will have to consider in making each of these orders, and the procedure you will go through if your case has to be decided in court.

What are the first steps I need to take in sorting out the finances?

You may be reading this passage having already been to see a solicitor, or you may not have got that far yet and are still just thinking about a divorce and what that would mean to you financially.

To begin with you need to gather as much information as you can to build up a picture of the finances in your marriage. If your house is owned, work out how much equity is in the property by calculating the rough value of the house, then taking away the outstanding mortgage. If you don't know what this figure is you can find out by asking the mortgage company. Make a note of all the bank accounts held by either you or your spouse, as well as any endowment policies, stocks, shares or other savings plans. Work out your total monthly income, including any wages you might earn, benefits you receive or income from any other sources, such as a pension payment, and do the same for your spouse's income. Then make a note of all your debts, whether they are for credit card purchases, bank loans, hire purchase agreements, catalogue purchases, mortgage arrears or anything else.

This will help your solicitor advise you as to what sort of settlement might be appropriate in your case. It is also likely to save time and costs if you can gather as much of this information as possible before your first discussion about the finances.

What if my husband has told me that I won't get anything out of the marriage?

It is very common, when a marriage breaks down, for one person to tell the other that they will end up getting nothing. A lot of threats are issued during a divorce and many women especially are told by their husbands that they will get nothing. Do not believe threats such as these as they are usually just designed to frighten you. Some men believe that if they threaten loudly enough their wives will just give up and agree to walk away with much less than they are entitled to.

It is important that you take proper advice at an early stage as to what sort of settlement you could expect were the matter to go to court. This way you will have a much better idea of what is a reasonable offer and what isn't. If your husband is not prepared to talk sensibly about the finances, and will not negotiate through his solicitor either, then it may be that you have no option other than to issue an application for the court to decide the financial issues.

What is a matrimonial asset?

It comes as a surprise to many of our clients, but the fact is (with a few exceptions) that any asset owned by either the husband or the wife individually, or assets that are held jointly, can be considered as assets of the marriage, or, as we say in legal jargon, they are 'matrimonial assets'. So, for example, if Mr Brown owned shares worth £15,000, and had £2000 cash in a bank account, Mrs Brown had an endowment policy worth £1500, and they had a house in their joint names worth £50,000, the total worth of the matrimonial assets would be £68,500. If the finances could not be agreed by the Browns and they went to court, a judge could re-allocate any of these assets in any way he thought appropriate, regardless of whose name they were in originally. So the shares could be given to Mrs Brown, the endowment policy and cash could go to Mr Brown, and the value of the house could be shared equally between them. Do not make the common mistake of thinking that just because a particular asset is in your spouse's name that means that you have no entitlement to it.

Here are two further examples.

Rhona

Rhona went to her solicitor with a serious dilemma. Her 13-year marriage had been on the rocks for some time, and she wanted desperately to get divorced. When asked what was stopping her, she said that she was terrified of becoming homeless because the house was in the sole name of her husband. Although they had been together when the house was bought, Rhona's husband had insisted that only his name should be on the title deeds. Now that the marriage was coming to an end, quite understandably Rhona was under the impression that the house would go to her husband as he was the legal owner of it.

In fact, although the house was in only the husband's name, it had been bought during the time of the marriage, and Rhona and her husband had lived in it together with their children for the last nine years. Because of these factors, the house was considered to be a 'joint matrimonial asset' and the fact that it was in her husband's name only made no difference at all. The end result of this particular case (without going into the smaller details) was that the house was eventually put on the market and Rhona received 60 per cent of the proceeds, which she was able to use as a deposit to buy a house for herself.

Catherine

Catherine was not worried when she first approached solicitors because she had a series of savings schemes in her sole name. Their total value was over £40,000 and Catherine was confident that she could easily use this as a deposit on a house. In this case there was very little else of any value in the marriage, and the judge thought it would be unjust for Catherine to have the full value of these policies while her husband received nothing, so he ordered that three of the savings plans (equalling just under half the total value) should be transferred to Catherine's husband.

While this was the proper outcome in this case, Catherine had not understood that even though the savings schemes were in her sole name, they could still be considered as matrimonial assets and redistributed by a judge between her and her husband to achieve a fair outcome.

In some ways it is not really fair to give you examples like the ones we have shown above, because you can't get a true picture of how the assets were split in any marriage without knowing the whole story. But the point you need to be aware of is that, just because a particular asset is in a sole name, that does not necessarily mean that it will end up going to the spouse who is the legal owner of it. In most cases, when you get divorced you need to take into account all the property that is in the name of either the husband or the wife or held jointly. These individual items then go into the 'pot' to make up the 'matrimonial assets', and it is all of these things together that will be taken into account when the final division is made.

What is a Schedule of Assets?

Unless you are in a situation where the finances can be agreed without any difficulty, your solicitor will need to make a complete list of all the money, assets and property that are owned jointly by you and your husband or held in your or his sole name. This includes any item that might be of value, including antiques, cars, the house (and any other property you might own), stocks, shares, and policies that have a cash value to them. Tell your solicitor about anything you think might be relevant and he will soon advise you as to whether it is valuable enough to be taken into account.

You will need to find the value of policies, shares or savings plans, which can be done by writing to the company and asking for the surrender value or cash equivalent transfer value (or CETV).

The document your solicitor prepares with this information is called the Schedule of Assets. He will use it to negotiate a fair division of the property with your spouse's solicitor, and it will be shown to the court should matters get that far.

All these things will take time, and my solicitor says it may be a few months until we get to court. What happens if I need money now?

You may well find yourself in a situation where you are desperately short of money following the break-up of a marriage, and you seem to be nowhere near reaching any sort of settlement as to the finances. What can you do in the short term? There are two immediate ways in which you might be able to ease the pressure before a final settlement is arrived at.

The first is to consider whether or not you might be entitled to state benefits considering the change in your circumstances. If you were not the main breadwinner in the house, and especially if you have children, you might find that there are benefits you can claim if you can show that you are no longer supported by your ex. While you may not want to go down the route of having to rely on benefits, you may find that doing so will help you, at least in the short term. It is worth both checking with your solicitor and also asking your local benefits office to see whether there are any benefits available that you qualify for. The new Working Tax Credit and Child Tax Credit (which replaced the Working Tax Families Tax Credit as from April 2003) can be especially helpful to people who have children living with them, and are now assessed for a period of 12 months at a time. See Chapter 11 for more information on state benefits.

The other temporary solution is to apply to the court for something known as Maintenance Pending Suit (or interim maintenance).

Maintenance Pending Suit

This is a maintenance order that is made to last until the finances are resolved permanently. Courts know that it can sometimes take several months for the finances to be sorted out, and a Maintenance Pending Suit order is designed to fill the gap between the breakdown of the marriage and the final financial order. You should note, however, that you can only apply for Maintenance Pending Suit once a divorce petition has been filed. It is not enough that you are living separately from your spouse.

Once you have applied for Maintenance Pending Suit you will need to show the court exactly what your monthly income is, as well as what your monthly outgoings are. If you can show that your income is not enough to cover your monthly needs, you stand a reasonable chance of being given Maintenance Pending Suit. However, you must also show that the expenses you have are reasonable ones, and also that your spouse has enough income to be able to make a contribution towards them. Even if your outgoings are entirely justified, your husband is unlikely to be able to contribute much to them if he is unemployed or on a very low income. If, however, he does have the ability to pay you maintenance in the short term, then a judge will assess your financial needs compared with his ability to pay, and order that he pays you a monthly amount until the finances can be permanently resolved.

The orders a court can make in financial proceedings

There are several different types of financial order that a judge can make in a financial case. He can make just one of these orders, or several of them, depending on the case and what is needed in it. What follows is a list of the main ones.

A Lump Sum Order

This is an order that one spouse pays a 'lump sum' of money to the other spouse. A lump sum can either be payable immediately (for example within 14 days) if the cash is already available, or at a later date if the money needs to be raised first, for example by selling property or when a policy matures on a future date.

A Periodical Payments Order

Periodical payments are basically another way of describing what you may know of as maintenance. It can be paid by either husband to wife or vice versa, but will usually depend on which person has the larger income, and whether one has supported the other during the marriage. Payments will normally be paid monthly, and a Periodical Payments Order can last either for a fixed term (i.e. for three years, or until a child starts full-time education and the mother can return to work) or alternatively can last for the 'joint lives' of the parties. This means that the periodical payments will stop only when either husband or wife dies, whichever occurs the sooner. There are certain other factors that will normally bring a Periodical Payments Order to an end. If, for example, it is the wife receiving periodical payments, then her payments will stop if she lives with another man for six months, or if she remarries.

Can the court order that my spouse pays periodical payments in respect of the children?

Since the arrival of the Child Support Agency, in most circumstances the court will not have the power to decide how much an absent parent should pay to maintain his children unless a figure has already been agreed between the parents themselves. In most cases, the parent who lives with the children will have to make an application (completely separate from the court proceedings) to the Child Support Agency, which will calculate how much the absent parent will have to pay.

However, there are a few exceptions to this rule, where the court can make an order for periodical payments in respect of a child. They include: cases where you are applying for payments from a step-parent, or someone who is not the natural parent of the child; cases where you require extra money to pay for school fees; cases in which a child has a disability and an extra allowance is needed for this; or situations where one of the parents is not resident in the UK. If you feel that your case might fall into one of these categories, then you should discuss with your solicitor the possibility of applying for periodical payments for the child (or children) through the courts.

A Property Adjustment Order

Property Adjustment Orders allow the court to transfer any property that is not cash (for example stocks, shares, policies or a house) from one spouse to another, or from joint names to the sole name of one of the parties. These orders are most common when the former matrimonial home (the house you last lived in together as husband and wife) is transferred to the sole name of one person following the break up of a marriage.

A Mesher Order

A Mesher Order can be used by the court to order that property is transferred from one party to the other (just as in a Property Adjustment Order), but at a later date. The most common example of this is where a wife is left living in the former matrimonial home with children.

It is not unusual for a judge to feel that the husband should be able to benefit from some of the money that is in the house, but that he does not want to order the house to be sold straightaway as the children are still living there and it would be wrong to deprive them of a home. In these cases, a judge might say that a lump sum should be paid to the husband, but only when the children finish full-time secondary education. Once this point is reached, the wife can then decide how the money should be paid. If she is able to raise the money by borrowing it or by saving it, then she can simply pay a lump sum over to her ex-husband. If she is not able to do either of these things, then she may still have to sell the house so that the husband can receive his proper share.

An Order for Sale

Within any financial proceedings following a divorce (or, as we refer to them, ancillary relief proceedings) a court also has the power to make an Order for Sale. This is most common in respect of the matrimonial home when the judge thinks that the only way to achieve a fair outcome for both parties in a case is for it to be sold and for both husband and wife to receive something from the proceeds.

A Pension Sharing Order

Relatively new laws regarding pensions mean that for any case where the divorce petition was filed after 1 December 2000, it is now possible to split a pension fund into two. So if, for example, your husband has a fund worth £100,000, the court has the power to create two entirely new pensions from this fund, one for the husband and one for the wife. The fund could be split equally so that each person receives a pension fund of £50,000, or it could be split any other way, for example £30,000 to one person and £70,000 to the other.

A Clean Break Order

The general view of the courts nowadays is that wherever possible they prefer to deal with financial disputes following a divorce in such a way that, once the order is made, the couple have no further responsibilities to each other and both are free to continue with their lives. When it can be achieved, this means that two people are not only free from any further financial burden to their ex-spouse, but can also move on emotionally. For this reason, you may find that, even where a Periodical Payments Order is justified, a court may prefer to avoid that by giving one person a greater share of the assets at the time of the divorce than they would otherwise receive. This then allows the other person to be free of any maintenance obligation. It is likely that if a court is presented with a clean break option that seems fair to both parties, then this will be an attractive option for any judge faced with making a final order.

The factors taken into account by a judge when deciding a financial case

As we have already said, it is impossible for anyone to make an exact prediction as to the outcome of any particular financial dispute, as judges have a lot of discretion in these cases. However, there are certain matters that a judge will have to take into account before making a final decision as to the outcome. A general principle is that the starting point for any judge considering a financial case is that the split should be 50:50.

However you will know from cases that you have read about that it is rarely as simple as a judge dividing all the assets in equal shares. There are many reasons why a judge will decide on an order that has moved away from the 50:50 principle to 60:40, or 66:34 (or any other division for that matter). The most common reason for giving one party a bigger share than the other is that he or she will become the parent with responsibility for looking after the children, and therefore has greater financial and housing needs than the other parent.

However it would be too simplistic to say that this is the only reason for deciding how the assets are divided, as there are many other factors that a judge must take into account:

1. The income of both parties to the marriage, as well as their potential for earning in the future.

(So, for example, if Mrs Smith who is 28 currently does not work because she looks after the children full time, it could be said that once the children are at school she will have a better chance of getting a job and therefore has potential to earn in the future. On the other hand, if Gladys is 57 and is partially disabled, the court is unlikely to expect her to go out and look for a job. A third example would be Sally, who currently does not earn anything because she is training to be an accountant. The court will see her as having a good earning potential in the future, and will take this into account when making a final order.)

2. Property and other financial resources that each of the parties has or is likely to acquire.

(A typical example here would be to take into account an endowment policy that was due to mature in two years' time. At the date of the court hearing it may only be worth £3,500, but it could pay out much more than this once it matures.)

3. The financial needs, obligations and resources of each of the parties.

(This heading covers many different points. Essentially the court would be interested in knowing the individual circumstances of both husband and wife. For example, Susan may need a car in order for her to do her job as a sales rep, which would be a relevant factor, and Bill may wish to point out that he still pays child maintenance in respect of a previous relationship, which will be an ongoing obligation for him.)

4. The standard of living that was enjoyed prior to the divorce.

(It is usually the case that once a marriage is over and the husband and wife go their separate ways, both of them have to take a slight drop in their standard of living, at least in the short term. However, the standard of living you have been used to is a relevant factor in deciding what your future needs and expectations are.)

5. The age of each party and the duration of the marriage.

(The younger the parties are, the more usual it is for a court to expect that they will both go on to lead their own independent lives and become self-supporting, so a 25-year-old would almost certainly be expected to take up some type of work eventually, while someone in their late 50s would not.

A court is also entitled to take into account if a marriage has been a very short one. In these cases a court is much more likely to be interested in what each party brought to the marriage in the beginning, rather than treating all property as a joint matrimonial asset and available for redistribution. For example, take a situation where Saskia and Jeremy split up after only two years of marriage, and Saskia already owned a house worth £50,000 prior to getting married. In this situation a court would be unlikely to split this property in equal shares, as this would be seen to be unfair on Saskia, but would be much more likely to give her the lion's share, if not all of the property's value. It would also be unlikely that the court would order a Periodical Payments Order for any great length of time. On the other hand, if two people had been married for 25 years, it is much more likely that all their property would be considered as available to split between them, and the courts would also take their long-term responsibilities to each other very seriously.)

6. Any physical or mental disability of either party to the marriage.

(Any disability that will affect either long-term job prospects, or means that one or other person has special needs because of the disability will be taken into account by the court. So, for example, if Mrs White had very bad arthritis and needed to live in a specially adapted bungalow, she would be able to argue in court that her financial needs may be more than they would have been had she been completely healthy.)

7. The contributions each party has made to the welfare of the family including looking after the home or caring for the family.

(Many men are of the view that if they have worked and earned a wage throughout the marriage and their wives have stayed at home with the children or as a housewife, then the wife should not be entitled to come away with an equal share of the assets. This is an old-fashioned view and one that will not find much sympathy with the courts. Unless there are exceptional circumstances, the general attitude of the courts is to treat the parties as if they have made equal contributions to the marriage.)

8. The conduct of each of the parties if it would be inequitable to disregard it.

(Many people going through a divorce feel very bitter about the break-up and do not see why there should be an equal share of the assets if it was their partner who in their view caused the split. The courts take the view nowadays that unless there are really exceptional circumstances, the conduct of either husband or wife will not be taken into account in relation to the financial settlement. Where conduct *is* taken into account, then it has to be both unusual and quite extreme. Having an affair or being generally unpleasant will not be considered as relevant. However, in a case where a husband had forged his wife's signature on several documents in order to cash in policies illegally, this was considered by the court to be the sort of conduct that was so bad that he should get less than he would have done otherwise.

9. The value of any benefit that a party will lose the chance of acquiring as a result of the divorce.

(This could apply to almost anything that either husband or wife could have expected had the marriage lasted. An example might be a lump sum payable on retirement that would have benefited both husband and wife but will now go to the husband only.)

Every case that reaches court will involve a different background, different assets, and parties with different needs, resources and expectations and, as we have already said, it is almost impossible for a lawyer or a book such as this to give a firm prediction as to what a particular judge would order in any particular case. Having said that, you should at least get some idea from the headings listed above as to the things that a judge will take into account when deciding any financial case before him, and this should help you both to prepare for court and to know your case's own strengths and weaknesses before getting there.

THE HOUSE

We have already gone through the factors that a court will take into account when deciding any financial case. For the vast majority of couples, though, the house they live in (or, as we lawyers like to call it, the 'former matrimonial home') is their biggest asset. Deciding who gets it or whether of not it should be sold is one of the hardest decisions that both divorcing couples and the courts are regularly faced with, so we thought it might be one area that is worth a little bit of individual attention.

How will I know which of us will get the house or whether it will have to be sold?

One of the biggest myths surrounding divorce is that it is always the woman who gets the house. Many men come to see solicitors absolutely convinced that if they get divorced they will end up homeless. This myth has no basis in reality because there is no hard and fast rule about who should get the house, or when it has to be sold.

The reason that this myth exists is that, more often than not, the children will remain living with the mother, and this is one of the main factors that helps courts decide who would end up getting the house. Lawyers are, of course, aware of this and are sometimes able to give their clients advice that will help them come to an agreement without having to go to court. For example, if Rita and Fred are about to get divorced, Fred might well be advised that if their three children are to remain living with their mother it would be fairer to let her stay with them in the house. He might then get a larger share of whatever assets are left over to compensate him for the fact that his former wife has kept the house.

Whatever your individual circumstances, there are certain questions you can ask yourself that might help you to understand where the house would be likely to go if the matter went to court. You can ask yourself the following questions regardless of whether you are male or female.

1. Are there any children in the marriage?

2. If so, have we decided which parent they are going to live with?

3. If we have decided that point, would that parent have any way of finding suitable accommodation if they couldn't stay in the house? (If the answer is no, it may well be that the parent with whom the children is living gets to stay in the house, at least until the children finish full-time education.)

4. How much are the monthly payments on the mortgage?

5. Would either of us be able to afford to keep those payments up on our own? (If the answer is no, the result may well be that the house will have to be sold.)

6. How big is the house? (Is it going to be too big for the needs of whichever person or people are left in it? If so, there may be an argument that the house should be sold and something smaller bought in its place.)

Factors that will help decide what happens to the house

The following section goes through some of the things a court would take into account if it had to make a ruling on what should happen to the house, but these factors are just as relevant to any couple faced with this decision. Any solicitor giving you advice on reaching an agreement with your ex should know what a court would be likely to do if the matter went that far, and should therefore be able to help you with deciding what would be likely to happen in your own individual case.

The needs of the children

The most important factor in deciding what should happen to the house is the children of the marriage. The court will want to make sure that the children have a stable home, at least until they finish full-time education. Therefore, if there are children in the marriage, it is often their needs that help decide which of the parents should stay living in the home.

The housing needs of both husband and wife

After the children, the court would then look at the needs of both the husband and wife themselves.

Until the end of the marriage, the house was able to provide a home for both of them. Once the marriage is at an end, a way has to be found of providing two homes instead of one. In many cases there simply isn't enough money in the marriage to buy two homes outright, so the court has to look for other ways round the problem and try to come up with a solution where both husband and wife will end up with a roof over their heads. Sometimes the answer is obvious and sometimes it is not.

It is important also to know that a 'housing need' means a need for stable, secure accommodation that provides a home, without needing to be luxurious. Lodging in a neighbour's spare room would not be considered suitable long-term housing, whereas living with a new partner in their house might well be. Just the same, an ex-wife with no children to look after would have trouble persuading a court that she should stay in a luxurious four-bedroom house unless there was enough cash available to house her ex-husband in similarly plush accommodation. This is because the court will look at what somebody *needs*, rather than what somebody would like to have. A single woman clearly does not need to live in a four-bedroom house on her own, especially if the husband has no cash with which to rehouse himself.

For example, if Bob has left his wife Sandra and is living with his new girlfriend in her house, Bob does not have an immediate housing need as he already has somewhere to live. However, if Bob had left his wife and was temporarily sleeping on a friend's floor, then he would be able to argue that he had a serious housing need, and any division of the property would have to take this need into account.

Looking at it in a slightly different way, if Pauline and Arthur live in a five-bedroom detached house worth £400,000 and they have no mortgage on the property (and for the sake of simplicity let's say they have no other assets), then its unlikely that a court would say that either Pauline or Arthur should get the house. The likely result is that the house would be put on the market, so that the proceeds could be used to buy both of them a smaller, less expensive property that would satisfy the housing needs of both of them.

The financial position of both husband and wife

The court will be interested to know how old each of the parties is, how much they are currently able to earn, and what potential they have for earning in the future. These things are all relevant in deciding the overall division of the assets, not just the house, but they cannot be forgotten when you are trying to make some headway on the house issue.

For example, Bill and Melanie live in a modest two-bedroom semi. Melanie is an advertising executive earning £35,000 a year with a degree in marketing, and Bill is a shop-worker earning £12,000 with no qualifications. In this case the court is likely to think that Melanie has a much better future earning potential than Bill. This also affects the size of mortgage that each of them will be able to get in the future. If the maximum mortgage is generally three and a half times a person's gross salary, then Bill would not be able to get much more that £42,000 on a mortgage whereas Melanie could probably raise about £120,000.

In this case, the court may think (and remember there are no hard and fast rules) that it would be fairer for Bill to remain living in the house, giving Melanie some of the other, smaller assets, because Melanie will find it much easier to rehouse herself in the future than Bill will. Both Melanie and Bill have a need for housing, but the house they live in can't be described as over-luxurious for Bill's needs, and Melanie will be able to rehouse herself because of her much higher salary.

In a case like this, you may wonder why the court doesn't just sell the house and divide the proceeds 50:50. Of course this does happen in quite a few cases, but in an example like this the proceeds of a two-bedroom semi would obviously not be enough to rehouse both

Melanie and Bill, so the court would be reluctant to sell it as it probably wouldn't get either of the parties any further forward. By selling it, the court would be able to give some of the cash to Melanie, which may seem fairer to her, but it would mean that Bill would be left without a home, and with his earnings he would also be in great difficulty when it came to rehousing himself. Letting him keep it and compensating Melanie in some other way is probably the fairest solution that a court could come up with in an imperfect world.

In fact this is one of the greatest problems when dividing the assets in any marriage. Apart from for those who are very wealthy, with enough money to provide comfortably for both husband and wife, most divorces lead to a situation where each has to 'start again'. Because of this, it is often the case that the best a judge can do is to try and find the solution that is fairest for both parties, taking all their relevant circumstances into account. Whatever the situation, a judge will always have at the forefront of his mind the fact that both parties from the marriage are going to need somewhere to live, and trying to come up with a solution that provides both parties with a realistic chance of finding stable accommodation as soon as possible will be one of the main factors in deciding any financial case.

THE COURT PROCESS

It is often the case that the only experience of the court system divorcing clients have ever had is on television. They will be used to seeing impressive and old-fashioned courtrooms full of barristers wearing wigs and gowns. The family courts are quite different to this. Financial matters are generally heard in the county court, not the Crown court where criminal matters are heard. In practice these two courts are often found in the same building, described as a 'combined court centre'.

Financial cases are often heard by district judges (often shortened to DJs!). They generally take place in fairly small rooms with a large table in the middle. The judge will sit on one side and the barristers and their clients will sit on the other. People do not stand except when they are taking the oath before giving evidence. There is no witness box or 'dock', and the whole room is much less formal than many of our clients expect.

The three-part system

In 2000 a new system was introduced in relation to sorting out financial matters at court. Be aware that if you discuss the court process with someone who divorced prior to this, their experience may well be quite different to yours.

There is also now something called a 'pre-action protocol', which is a set of guidelines for how cases should be handled by solicitors prior to going to court. The general idea is to promote the making of settlements between parties without the need for going to court wherever this is possible. For example, it is suggested that the first letter written by one solicitor to another in financial proceedings should not be hostile and aggressive, as this approach is only likely to inflame the situation and make any agreement less probable. You should be able to see and approve this letter before it is sent to your ex's solicitor. Good solicitors should reply promptly (within a maximum of 14 days) to any letters in relation to settling the finances, and should also avoid dragging out the negotiations for too long if it looks as though an agreement will not be reached.

Once you have reached the stage where you think that going to court cannot be avoided, you need to issue an Application for Ancillary Relief by filing what is known as a Form A. Your solicitor will take care of this paperwork for you. Once the Form A has been filed with the court, this sets in motion an automatic timetable that will go right through to the Final Hearing. The First Appointment at court will be between 12 and 14 weeks following the date you filed the Form A.

You will also be required to fill in what is known as a Form E. This is a long form (about 20 pages) requiring all sorts of details about your finances, any assets of the marriage, any property owned, and details of all your income, needs, expenditure and debts. You will have to attach various things to your Form E, such as recent payslips and bank statements.

The idea is that your spouse will also fill in a Form E, and that both documents will be exchanged simultaneously not less than 35 days prior to the First Appointment. Again, your solicitor will make sure that this happens, and if for any reason it does not, he should chase the other side to see where their Form E has got to.

Two weeks prior to the First Appointment, both sides must file certain documents with the court, including:

a. A statement of the issues between the parties

(This document just explains what both sides are asking the court to do, highlighting the areas that are not in agreement, such as whether or not a property should be sold, or whether a pension should be split.)

b. A chronology

(This is a document that includes the dates of all events that are relevant to the marriage, such as the marriage itself, the birth of any children, a party being made redundant, the date of separation etc.)

c. A questionnaire

(The questionnaire is a list of any further documents or questions that you have prior to the court hearing that would help clarify the financial situation of your ex-spouse. You might ask what a particular bank loan is in respect of, or what certain transactions on a bank account statement refer to.)

c. A Form G

(This form asks whether you would be in a position to miss out the First Appointment stage and have a Financial Dispute Resolution hearing instead. Both these hearings are explained in the following paragraphs.)

Once your case is ready to proceed to court, there are three types of hearing that you may have to attend. They are the First Appointment, the Financial Dispute Resolution Hearing, and the Final Hearing.

The First Appointment

The title of this hearing explains what it is – the first time that your financial case is listed at court. The First Appointment is usually very short, about 10–15 minutes, and either your solicitor or someone else from the firm will usually represent you at this stage.

The purpose of this hearing is really to set the wheels in motion in the case. No final decisions can be made by a judge at this hearing and no one gives evidence at it. The main reason for being at court is to make sure that everything is on track for the case to be heard at a later date. The judge can make what are called 'directions'; these are matters that must happen by a specific date in order for the case to proceed. For example, if you have requested more detailed information from the other side and you have not yet received it, this is the hearing where this can be mentioned. The judge can then order that your questions are answered by a specific date. If statements are to be needed from witnesses who are likely to be called at the Final Hearing, then the judge can direct that this should happen in good time.

The First Appointment is also an opportunity for both legal representatives to meet outside the courtroom, to see if there is any room for further negotiation: some clients are put off by the court process, and will do almost anything to avoid the matter having to go through to a Final Hearing; as time goes on, people's individual circumstances change, and they might, for whatever reason, be more willing to try to come to some sort of compromise. If this is possible then a good solicitor will take this opportunity to discuss matters with the other side. If there is clearly no possibility that the matter might settle, then the case is listed for the next type of hearing, known as the Financial Dispute Resolution, or as we like to shorten it, the FDR.

The Financial Dispute Resolution Hearing

This type of hearing is a recent invention designed to save court time and encourage people to settle matters, wherever this is possible, without having to go on to a Final Hearing (in something like 50 per cent of cases the parties manage to come to an agreement at the FDR stage). The format varies slightly between different courts, but the principles remain broadly the same.

As a general rule, the parties themselves (that is you and your ex-spouse) do not give evidence themselves. The reason we say 'as a general rule' is that a few judges like to do things in their own way and, if there is a matter that concerns them, they sometimes like to ask one of the parties themselves about it. However, this is not the general purpose of the FDR hearing.

The FDR is in fact made up of two hearings, each lasting between 15 and 30 minutes. The idea is that both legal representatives (often barristers by this stage) present the case to the judge and give her a nutshell outline of both the case and the outcome that their clients would wish for. For example, a barrister might say something along these lines in a simple case:

'I represent Mrs Smith. This was a 15-year marriage that ended when the parties separated in April of last year. There is one child of the marriage, Gemma who is five years old and lives with her mother. There are only limited assets in the marriage, which total £65,000 in value. The first is the former matrimonial home at 22, Eden Crescent. The mother has been living there with Gemma since separation. The property has recently been valued at £125,000 and there is an outstanding mortgage of £75,000, leaving equity of £50,000.

My client proposes that the property be transferred to her outright so that she has a home for herself and her daughter. The only other asset is a joint savings account with a current balance of £15,000. Mrs Smith proposes that she pays £5000 of this to Mr Smith and keeps the balance. She is willing on that basis to forgo (go without) any maintenance from her former husband. Mr Smith has a far greater earning potential than she does, as he earns £25,000, whereas Mrs Smith only earns £12,000 a year. It is therefore Mrs Smith's position that she wishes the court to transfer the property to her.'

This, of course, is a very over-simplified example. Mrs Smith's barrister puts forward the proposal to the judge that the property (and therefore an asset worth £50,000) goes to her outright. In addition she would receive £10,000 from the savings account, leaving Mr Smith with only £5000 out of the total of £65,000.

Once this 'speech' has been made, it is then the turn of Mr Smith's barrister who might say something along these lines:

'I represent Mr Smith, who is of the view that the best outcome would be for the property to be sold and the proceeds split 50:50 between the parties. He also sees no reason why the joint savings account should not also be split so that both Mr and Mrs Smith receive £7500 from it. Although his last year's pay shows earnings of £25,000, in fact this is nowhere near his normal earnings as last year he had much more overtime than usual. His basic pay is in fact only £13,500 a year. Therefore he feels that he should not have to pay any maintenance to Mrs Smith as their earnings are not very far apart with him earning £13,500 and Mrs Smith earning £12,000. Mr Smith's proposal therefore is that the house be sold immediately and that each of the parties receives £32,500 of the total amount available.'

Once both barristers (or solicitors) have had their turn, the judge will make some comments as to what she thinks the likely outcome of the case will be. She will also be aware of any offers that have been made between the parties in correspondence. For instance, she may say:

'Having heard both barristers and having considered the assets available in this case, if I were deciding this case today, I would not be keen to order that the property be sold, bearing in mind that Gemma is still only five and needs a secure home in which to live. However, I also do not think it right that Mr Smith should leave this marriage with only £5000 of the assets, which is what Mrs Smith is suggesting should happen. My view is that the house should be transferred to Mrs Smith, and that all the money in the joint account, i.e. £15,000, should be paid to Mr Smith. I also think it would be appropriate for Mr Smith to pay a small amount of maintenance to Mrs Smith for a fixed period, say the next three years at a rate of something like £200 per month. I do not have the power to make a final order today unless the parties agree to it, but I hope that my comments have given you some help and guidance as to what another judge might do at a Final Hearing.'

The important point to note here is that judge at an FDR hearing does not have the power to make a final order, *unless both parties consent to it*. What she can do, which is in fact the whole purpose of the FDR, is to give a hint as to what would be the likely outcome following a Final Hearing. As you can see from the above example, the judge can either go along with one of the proposals put forward, or can come up with a totally different suggestion, which perhaps neither of the parties had thought of prior to the FDR hearing.

What happens next is that everybody is sent out of the courtroom, and both Mr and Mrs Smith have a chance to talk to their barristers about what was said in court. The barristers can then get together to see whether there is any chance of settling the matter, given what the judge has just said.

It might be that both Mr and Mrs Smith hate the judge's proposal, and both tell their barristers that they will not agree to it. If that is the case then obviously no agreement can be reached. On the other hand, Mr Smith might come to the view that no judge would be likely to order that the house be sold, especially as Gemma is so young, so he will settle for the £15,000 in the joint savings account. Although he doesn't want to pay maintenance, he is relieved that it would only be for three years, and he knows that he will be able to find enough overtime to raise £200. If this is the case, he might tell his barrister that he could go along with what the judge has proposed.

Mrs Smith might also be relieved that the house would be hers as this was her main concern, and she might accept advice from her barrister that any judge would be unlikely to give Mr Smith as little as £5000 out of the total available. She might also be encouraged by the fact that she would have £200 per month that she had not even asked for!

When this happens, or at least when clients like Mr and Mrs Smith start to get nearer to a settlement than they have been up to that time, the barristers spend some time talking first to their client and then again to the other side. As a result of these discussions, if an agreement is reached, the two barristers draw up a document confirming in writing what has been agreed and ask to go back in to see the judge. They tell the judge that an agreement has been arrived at (otherwise known as a Consent Order), the judge checks that she is happy with it, and agrees to make it a formal order of the court.

This order is then binding; it will be typed up into a formal court document and sent to both sets of solicitors within a few days of the order being made, and that is then the end of the matter as no further hearing is needed.

On the other hand, if Mr and Mrs Smith find themselves completely unable to come to any form of agreement, despite what the judge has said, the two barristers will go back before the judge, explain that this is the case, and she will then just list the matter for the Final Hearing, when the final decision will be made. It is also important to note that the judge who heard the FDR is not then able to hear the Final Hearing. This is because the FDR is designed so that both sides can talk openly and show any offers they have made to the judge. At the Final Hearing, these offers are kept private until the end of the case (see Legal Costs and Calderbank Offers, pages 96–97) so it must be heard by a different judge from the one who was present at the FDR.

The Final Hearing

As you would expect from the title, the Final Hearing is just that – the last hearing on the financial issues, where it is expected that a final and binding decision will be made as to what should happen to all the financial and property issues in the marriage.

This hearing is different from the previous two, and will be listed for a time period that the legal representatives feel will be long enough to deal with all the issues and hear all the evidence in the case. Each 'half day' period that the case is listed for is in fact roughly two and a half hours, as the courts generally sit from 10.30am until 1pm and then again from 2pm until 4.30pm. You will see from the documents that you receive about the date of the Final Hearing how long your case is listed for.

Straightforward cases where no witnesses are to be called can usually be easily dealt with in less than a day of court time. If, however, there are a large amount of assets, complex business accounts involved, or witnesses to be called, then the case may well take longer than a day.

The format of the hearing as we outline it should be used as a guide only, because district judges have a lot of discretion as to how they go about hearings in their own court. Some keep silent throughout the whole proceedings, giving judgement only at the end, while others take a much more active role and ask questions directly of the clients all the way through!

The general format, however, is that the barrister representing the Petitioner speaks first, usually for no more than a few minutes, outlining the background to the case by referring to the chronology, telling the judge what all the assets are, and giving a brief summary of his client's case.

He will then go on to 'call' his client to give evidence. This means that the Petitioner takes an oath, either by swearing on the Bible or, if they prefer, by making what is known as an 'affirmation', i.e. making a promise to the court that they will tell the truth. The barrister then asks the Petitioner to confirm that the contents of any statements that have been filed are true, and goes on to ask a series of questions about the case. Again, it is impossible to say how much detail your barrister will need to go into with you. Sometimes the issues are fairly simple and obvious: at other times they need a great deal more explanation.

A judge can intervene at any time if he chooses, either by asking to clarify something or by asking a question that your barrister may not have thought of. When your barrister has finished asking questions (and remember your barrister is on your side, so is not trying to trip you up or confuse you; if this happens, he or she is not doing their job properly), it is then the turn of your ex's barrister to ask you questions. This is called cross-examination. Most clients do not know that there are rules about how a barrister can ask questions, depending on who is being asked.

If a barrister is asking his own witness (i.e. you) questions, then he can't do this in a 'leading' way. He must ask open questions, such as 'what happened next' or 'how much do you earn, and how much of this is overtime?'. On the other hand, if you are being cross-examined, expect to be asked questions in a very different way. Leading questions are allowed in this situation, so that the barrister can quite properly say 'you have recently spent £5000 on a leather, settee haven't you?' or 'you have as much overtime available as you want every month, don't you?'.

Remember that the barrister will only have got his information from what he has been told by his client, i.e. your ex, so you should have some idea of what is coming prior to the hearing just by thinking through what you ex is likely to have said to his legal representative. When you are being cross-examined, take your time with each answer. It can be very easy to agree with a statement put by a skilled barrister when you don't really agree with what is said at all. If you don't understand the question, ask the barrister to repeat it, and if you feel that you have not explained yourself properly, ask for the opportunity to explain it again. The evidence that you give at this stage is very important, as it will help the judge in coming to his decision. He will be listening to your evidence and also making his own private judgement as to how believable you are. If he thinks you are lying about one part of the evidence, it may mean that he does not believe you later on when in fact you are telling the truth!

At the end of cross-examination, your own barrister can 're-examine' you, i.e ask more questions, but only on anything new that came up when the other barrister had his turn with the questions. After this the barrister will ask the judge whether he has any questions and, if not, that is the end of your evidence.

At this point, if you have any witnesses (most financial cases do not need any apart from the parties themselves) they will be called to give evidence on your behalf. When that has been done it will be the Respondent's turn to give evidence. As with your turn, he will be asked questions first by his barrister and then be cross-examined by yours.

When all the evidence is over, both barristers will give a speech that sums up the case for their client, highlighting anything relevant that has come out in evidence by one or other or both of the parties. They will each ask the judge to make the orders that their clients would like, and sometimes will present two alternatives to the judge so that he has different options that would favour you both.

At the end of these speeches, the judge will make his judgement. Sometimes he will go straight on to the judgement, sometimes he will ask for a few minutes to clear his thoughts and write some notes, and in complicated cases, or if it is very late in the day, he might even suggest that the judgement is given on another day. This is known as 'reserving judgement'.

Once the judgement has started, it is not appropriate for either the barristers or the clients themselves to speak at this point. If something in the judgement is wrong or needs clarifying, this can be done at the end of the judge's speech. Trying to interrupt him during a judgement will be guaranteed to annoy him, which will not help the case at all! The judgement will tell you the final decision as to what should happen to the assets, whether the house should be sold or transferred to one of the parties, whether there should be maintenance and if so in what amount and for how long. Whether or not you feel the judgement is in your favour, you should at least have a clear idea at the end of it as to what is to happen.

LEGAL COSTS AND CALDERBANK OFFERS

During the course of the negotiations that have led up to the Final Hearing, your solicitor should have made offer(s) to the other side on your behalf in an attempt to settle matters. These offers are often known as 'Calderbank offers', named after a couple called Mr and Mrs Calderbank whose case decided this principle. The judge will not have seen these Calderbank offers (from either side) at any time either before or during the hearing. If, at the end of the day, the judgement that is made is at least as favourable, or more favourable to you than any offer you have made, you may be entitled to receive some of your legal costs from the other side.

For example, say that a husband and wife had a total of £20,000 to split between them. On 1 January Mrs Smith asks her solicitor to write to the other side to say that she will accept £10,000 as being her fair share of the available money. Mr Smith will not accept this offer, and eventually the matter goes to court on 15 May.

After the Final Hearing, the judge decides that, because of all the evidence he has heard, he thinks that Mrs Smith should get £10,500 of the money, i.e more than she was prepared to accept in the first place. He does not know that she made an offer back in January so, at the end of the case, Mrs Smith's barrister finds a copy of the letter and shows it to the judge. The judge can then make a further award to Mrs Smith, because she has 'beaten her offer' in court, and he can decide that Mr Smith has to pay some or all of her legal costs. Often a judge will decide that Mr Smith will have to pay any legal costs that were incurred after the offer was made, i.e. after 1 January. As this amount will include all the fees involved in the Final Hearing, it is obviously an order worth having.

Of course, this Calderbank principle can work both for you and against you, so remember that if an offer is made by the other side prior to the Final Hearing, and you feel it is a realistic offer of settlement, it may well be worth considering whether or not you should accept it. If you don't and it is your ex who ends up beating his offer in court, then it should be you who is faced with a hefty legal bill that means that you end up with even less money than you thought you would. Quite apart from the money side of things, there are not many people who take much emotional satisfaction from having to pay their ex's legal costs! If your solicitor or barrister starts talking to you about 'being vulnerable on the costs issue' or 'the other side having made a good Calderbank offer', first ask them to explain the situation properly, then ask for clear advice as to whether they think you still have a realistic chance of doing better than the offer should the matter go through to a Final Hearing.

SOME ADDITIONAL QUESTIONS

The house is in the sole name of my husband. Do I still have a claim on it?

The 'legal owner' of any property is the person (or people) whose name is on the deeds. You will probably know whether or not you are a joint owner of your home, because if you are you will have been involved with all the paperwork when it was bought.

Most couples decide to buy their home together and become the joint legal owners of it, but there are some situations where the marital home is in the name of only the husband or the wife. This may be because the house was bought prior to the relationship starting, or because either husband or wife was already linked to another mortgage and unable to buy another property. Sometimes this situation can come about because one person simply does not wish to enter into a joint purchase with another person, and thinks that by keeping it in their sole name they can prevent problems at a later date.

Do not think that if the house is in your husband's sole name this means that you have no claim to it. As explained earlier, the general rule following a divorce (unless it has been a very short marriage) is that any property owned by either husband or wife becomes a matrimonial asset, regardless of who the legal owner is. This means that it can be considered as something that is part of the total amount available to split between you.

Even if our home is a matrimonial asset, can't my husband still sell it without telling me if he is the sole legal owner?

In theory the answer to this question is yes. Any person who owns something is free to sell it without the consent of anyone else. Having said that, if you think there is a chance your husband might try and sell the marital home without your knowledge or consent, you can protect yourself by asking your solicitor to do something known as 'registering your interest'. This means that when your husband comes to try and sell the property and the buyer's solicitors do all the normal checks on it, they will find out that you have an interest in the property, and your husband will be prevented from selling it without your consent. Solicitors are used to dealing with this type of problem, so if you are in a situation where the house is owned solely by your spouse, make sure you let your solicitor know this as soon as possible.

My husband inherited some money just before the divorce. Will this be treated as a matrimonial asset as well?

Earlier in the chapter we explained how all assets, whether owned by husband or wife, will in normal circumstances be treated as 'matrimonial assets' available for division between the parties. The business of inheritance is a slightly more tricky issue, in that the courts are less willing to treat an inheritance in exactly the same way as other assets within a marriage.

Although there is certainly no hard and fast rule about how an inheritance should be treated, the courts are generally reluctant to order that an inheritance should be split 50:50, however it still remains something that the court can consider as being relevant to the question of the needs and resources of each of the parties. Having said that, an inheritance will nevertheless (in normal circumstances) be treated slightly differently from the other assets available for division. The reason for this is that the courts view an inheritance as being more personal to a particular individual than almost any other asset, in that it is obvious that the person who died intended the money or property to be left to that person and not someone else. For that reason, the court will often either disregard an inheritance when dividing the assets, or will give a significantly larger share of it to the party whose inheritance it was.

A related problem arises when the husband (for example) argues that his wife will soon come to benefit from money or property through an inheritance. He may feel that a large sum of money just round the corner should be up for grabs just like everything else. Courts, however, tend to find this approach distasteful, as inheritances inevitably rely on someone dying, which is something that judges do not enjoy speculating upon in the courtroom. Unless the death is so imminent, or the sum of money expected so large that it would be simply unfair to ignore it, you are unlikely to have much success if you are asking a judge for a share of an inheritance that has not yet materialised. A future inheritance will, however, in the same way as an existing inheritance does, have some relevance to the question of your spouse's future needs, and the judge may take this into account when dividing up the assets that are available at the date of the hearing. (An interesting final note here is that the one other matter treated as being more personal than a general matrimonial asset is any money received as a result of a compensation or personal injury claim.)

What should I do if I think my wife is going to spend all our money before we reach a settlement on the finances?

If you are seriously concerned that your spouse is planning to either withdraw money, cash in policies, sell shares, or otherwise dispose of assets from the marriage, then you can apply to the court for an order to stop this happening. You must tell your solicitor immediately if this is a concern, as your spouse is unlikely to wait for long if she is intending to dispose of the assets.

If you can persuade the court that there is a real risk of this happening, then it can grant an injunction that will either order your wife not to sell or dispose of a particular item, or alternatively will hand over the money in question to an independent person who will look after it until a final decision is made about who it should go to.

If a person has already tried to dispose of an asset (for example by signing it over to someone else) you should inform your solicitor without delay; a court can in some circumstances 'set aside' such transactions.

What does it mean to 'capitalise maintenance?'

Earlier in the chapter we explained that one of the options open to a judge was to order that your ex-spouse pay you periodical payments, or maintenance. On the other hand, we also explained that wherever possible, judges prefer to make a Clean Break Order, where neither party will have any further obligation towards the other.

One way of dealing with this problem in a case where you would be entitled to periodical payments (or maintenance), is to 'capitalise' your maintenance. This simply means that, instead of receiving regular payments for a certain number of years or for your joint lives (if this is appropriate), you receive a big lump sum up-front to compensate you for going without the maintenance you would otherwise have got.

One important point to note about this principle, though, is that a court does not have the power to order that someone capitalises maintenance unless both parties agree both to the principle of it and to the sum that has to be paid. So, for example, if Jean thinks that a judge might order that she receive maintenance of £200 per month for the next five years, this would amount to £12,000 over the whole period. Peter might then offer to pay £10,000 as a lump sum up-front, thereby 'capitalising' the maintenance. Although this is less than the total £12,000 Jean would have received, she has the advantage of receiving the whole amount up-front rather than having to wait for it, whereas Peter has the advantage of being free from any further obligation towards Jean.

If both parties agree to this as a way forward, then the judge can make this into an order, and will be able to reach a clean break settlement. However, if either Jean or Peter is not happy with this arrangement, the judge would not have the power to make the order, and so a clean break may not be possible in this situation. In any situation where a maintenance order is a likely outcome, it is worth considering whether it would be possible to raise enough money to make an offer of capitalising the maintenance, as this can have advantages for both sides.

CHAPTER 8

THE CHILDREN

One of the most traumatic things about getting divorced – and indeed the reason many people avoid it for so long – can be making long-term decisions about the children; where they should live, which parent they should live with, how often the other parent should have contact with them and how to go about arranging this.

Statement of Arrangements

You will already have read in Chapter 5 that whichever person files the divorce petition (the person who starts off all the proceedings) is also asked to fill in a document called the Statement of Arrangements. This document asks lots of questions about the plans that the Petitioner has for all sorts of matters relating to the children's welfare. We have decided not to reproduce the whole form here, as in total it is about eight pages long, but these are some of the questions that the form includes.

Home details

Give the address at which each child lives.

Give details of the number of living and bedrooms etc. at the above address.

Is the house rented or owned, and if so by whom?

Is the rent or mortgage being regularly paid?

Give the names of all other persons living with the children. State their relationship with the children.

Will there be any change in these arrangements?

Education and training details

Give the names of schools/colleges attended by each child.

Do the children have special educational needs?

Will there be any change in these arrangements?

Childcare

Which parent looks after the children day to day?

Does that parent go out to work?

Does someone look after the children when that parent is not there?

Who looks after the children in the school holidays?

Will there be any change in these arrangements?

Maintenance

Does your husband/wife pay towards the maintenance of the children?

Is the payment made under a court order?

Is the payment following an assessment by the Child Support Agency?

Has maintenance for the children been agreed?

Details for contact with the children

Do the children ever see your husband/wife?

Will there be any change to these arrangements?

Give details of proposed arrangements for contact and residence.

Details of health

Are the children generally in good health?

Do they have any special health needs?

Other court proceedings

Are the children in the care of the local authority or under the supervision of a social worker?

Are any of the children on the Child Protection Register?

Are there, or have there been any proceedings in any court involving the children, for example adoption, custody/residence, access/ contact, care, supervision or maintenance?

What the court is trying to establish

You will see from the nature of the questions above that the court is concerned to know whether there is agreement by both parents on all the vital issues affecting the children and their upbringing.

When the Petitioner fills in this form, a copy will be sent to the Respondent so that he can see what all the answers are. When the proceedings reach the stage where the judge decides whether or not you should be granted a decree nisi (see page 57), he will then go on to see whether or not he thinks that the proposed arrangements for the children are satisfactory. If he does, then he will give both parties a certificate showing this. This is an important certificate, as without it your decree absolute (or final divorce) may be delayed. If the judge is not satisfied with the information on the Statement of Arrangements, then he can deal with this in several different ways: he can ask for more information from either or both of the parties, he can ask for a welfare report, or in some cases he can even ask to see the parties in court.

Resolving the issues

The best way of resolving any issues over the children is of course for both parents to be able to agree between themselves what the best outcome should be. It is also worth considering whether mediation may be able to help you talk things through with your spouse and come to some sort of agreement that benefits the children and that you can both live with (see Chapter 6).

Sometimes, however, the situation arises where two people simply aren't able to reach an agreement, so that matters eventually end up being resolved by a judge in court. While it is very unusual for the divorce itself to lead to a contested court hearing, it is not at all unusual for ex-spouses to end up at court over issues to do with either money or the children.

Court orders

There are basically four types of order that a court is able to make in relation to the children:

- Residence Orders
- Contact Orders
- Prohibited Steps Orders
- Specific Issue Orders

A Residence Order decides which person the children should live with. It is possible for a court to make a joint Residence Order, though these are fairly uncommon. A Contact Order defines how often a child should have contact with the absent parent and for how long. It can also state whether this contact should be supervised, unsupervised, direct (i.e. face to face), or indirect (i.e. letters and cards). Prohibited Steps and Specific Issue Orders both deal with any decisions that could normally be taken by a person with parental responsibility for a child (see page 131). They are explained more fully at the end of the chapter.

Do I have to have a court order in relation to the children?

No you don't. In many cases parents are able to agree all the important decisions concerning their children either between themselves or through solicitors or mediation, and never need to go to court over them. In these situations it is not necessary to have a court order. An order will only become necessary when agreement can't be reached or when either or both people want the agreement to be written down and made formal by the court.

Is it common to have to go to court over residence (or custody)?

It is important that we reassure you that although lawyers are used to dealing with residence issues on a regular basis, in fact residence hearings are only necessary in a very small proportion of all divorce cases. There is a strong likelihood that you will be able to come to a joint decision about where the children should live without ever having to go through the court system.

RESIDENCE (OR CUSTODY)

Custody is the old-fashioned term for describing where the children should live. You will often hear people describing cases where a parent 'had to fight for custody'. In fact nowadays lawyers and courts refer to issues of 'residence' rather than use the word custody.

What happens if we can't decide who the children should live with?

If the parents are able to agree between themselves where the children should live then so much the better, but if there is no agreement one of the parents will need to issue something known as a 'residence application'. This simply means filling in a form saying that you wish the court to make an order that the child/children should reside with you, and giving brief reasons why you think this should happen. Once you have done this you will also have to file a statement that sets out your reasons in more detail than the original form.

What should I include in my statement?

Both you and the other parent will be allowed to file statements prepared by your solicitors saying why you each think the children should live with you. You can include any issues that are relevant to your particular family, so your statement will touch on where both parents live, the standard of accommodation, whether you work, and if so for how long, any childminding arrangements you might need, and where the children have been used to living and going to school. You would also mention if any of the children has any special educational or health needs, and how each parent could provide for these needs if the children were to live with them.

Statements in residence applications often also touch on how involved each parent has been with the children's upbringing before they separated, the standard of that care and also whether the children have said either way where they would prefer to live.

Filing the statements

The statements that you file will be prepared by your solicitor when she has had a chance to talk to you about your situation, your views on where the children should be living and why. Don't be afraid to tell your solicitor anything that you think might be relevant to your residence application. Remember that she has never met the other members of your family, or seen where or how you live, so explain as much to her about your domestic circumstances as you think might be relevant. In the statement she will include the things she thinks a judge would be interested in knowing about, and she will know from experience which matters to put in and which to leave out, so don't be concerned if your solicitor has not included every tiny detail in the statement she has prepared on your behalf.

Once these statements have been filed by both you and your ex-partner or husband there is likely to be a preliminary short hearing at court (called a directions hearing) at which the judge appoints a family court adviser. Family court advisers (they used to be called welfare officers, so some people might still refer to them in this way) are people with a background in either probation or social work. Their responsibility is to take a completely independent view of the situation (they are not instructed or employed by either the mother or the father; they work directly for the court) and to make recommendations as to what, in their view, would be in the best interests of the child.

How do family court advisers go about writing their reports?

Family court advisers have a lot of discretion as to how they go about compiling their report, but in general you can expect them to see both parents in addition to any other important family members, to visit both homes, and to see the children face to face unless they are particularly young. In some cases they will also wish to see the children in the company of each parent so that they can see for themselves how each parent interacts with the children.

Once all their inquiries are complete, the family court adviser will write a report that recommends where the child should live. This document is by no means binding on the court, but it is fair to say that in the majority of cases the court will go along with what the family court adviser recommends, unless there are very strong reasons for not doing so.

It quite often happens that at some stage during the proceedings one of the parents has a change of heart and decides not to continue with the fight over residence. This can happen for a number of different reasons, but often residence applications are started because divorces are painful, and the thought of not living with your children can be a very hard one to accept. Parents can also feel that they do not want to give up the chance of living with the children 'without a fight'. Often though, when looked at objectively, it can become much clearer as to where the children's best interests lie in terms of residence, and the parents can then turn their attention to sorting out issues over contact. If this is not the case, however, once all the relevant statements are filed, and the family court adviser has compiled his report, the case will be listed for a Final Hearing in front of a judge.

What if serious allegations are being made?

In some cases, once issues over either residence or contact are started, one or both parents will make serious allegations against the other. These might involve domestic violence, cruelty towards the children or sometimes even sexual abuse. A family court adviser reading these allegations is very rarely in a position to make up his own mind as to where the truth lies, especially if one person is insisting that something happened and the other denies it completely. In these situations the judge sometimes suggests there should be something called a 'perpetration hearing' before a final decision on residence can be made. This means that there will be a separate court hearing to look at the allegations on their own and decide whether or not, in the view of the court, they can be proved either way.

Although having a perpetration hearing sounds like an easy solution when there are allegations flying around, in truth the hearing often ends up being one person's word against another, and it can sometimes be almost impossible for the court to decide where the truth lies. Because of this, some judges are far less keen than others to go down the perpetration hearing route, and it would be impossible to predict in a book like this which cases will lead to a perpetration hearing and which will not. That will depend on the type of allegations that are being made, and whether a particular judge feels that a perpetration hearing would be likely to help resolve what actually happened.

It is important to know that if there is a perpetration hearing, say on an allegation of violence, and the judge makes a 'finding' that the violence did occur, then the family court adviser from that point on has to act as though what the judge has found is the true version of events, whatever his own opinion of the evidence might be. A 'finding' is in some ways like a 'verdict' would be in a criminal case, in that the judge is making a decision one way or the other as to what did or did not happen.

If that sounds a bit confusing then take this example:

Alison and Tony

This divorcing couple are arguing over where the children, Lucy (6) and Victoria (3), should live. When Alison produces her statement, she says in it that Tony would never be a good father to the children because he used to smack them regularly and on one occasion hit Lucy so hard that her legs were bruised. Tony, in his statement says that this is all lies and that Alison has made these things up just to get back at him for seeing another woman.

The family court adviser does not know where the truth lies and the judge orders that there should be a perpetration hearing. At the hearing, both Alison and Tony give evidence, and the judge makes a 'finding' that Alison is telling the truth and that her statement is the true version of events, not Tony's.

From this point on, the family court adviser must treat the findings of the judge as though they represent the truth. Of course, a hearing such as this could go either way, but it allows the family court adviser to make a recommendation on a firm basis, rather than wondering whether Alison or Tony's version of events is the right one.

Unfortunately there are cases where allegations are made, sometimes quite serious ones, and the judge comes to the view that he does not have enough evidence to decide the matter either way, and it can be quite difficult for both parents when allegations like these are left unresolved. In these situations, the family court adviser simply has to make the best recommendation he can in the light of the facts that are known. Once the perpetration hearing is over (if one was needed) the case can then move on to the Final Hearing.

THE FINAL HEARING

Once the family court adviser has written and submitted his report (often called the welfare report), a copy is given to both sides, and the case can proceed to court. The hearing will be in private, so members of the public will not be allowed in. Barristers or solicitors will not be wearing wigs or gowns and the hearing itself can be either in the judge's room (called chambers) or in a courtroom, depending on the number of witnesses involved.

The family court adviser will sometimes give evidence first, and on other occasions will stay to the end of the hearing, listen to what the parties have to say in evidence, and then give his views at the end. Whether he goes first or last depends on the custom of that particular court, the views of the judge, and whether the recommendation is a strong one or quite finely balanced either way. In either event, both legal representatives will have a chance to cross-examine the family court adviser as to the recommendations in the report and why he has reached those views.

Both parents will also have a chance to give evidence, as will any witnesses they have decided to call to support their case. Before giving evidence you will be expected either to take an oath on the Bible (or other religious text) or make what is known as an affirmation (a promise to the court to tell the truth) if that is what you would rather do. During your evidence you should think before answering any questions, and do not be afraid to ask for a question to be repeated if you didn't understand it properly the first time.

At the end of all the evidence the judge will listen to final speeches (or closing submissions, in legal jargon) from both solicitors or barristers, and will go on to make a decision as to where the children should live. Any hearing on residence may very well also be linked to applications on contact, and it is likely that the judge will go on to decide how often the parent who will not be living with the children should have contact with them.

How does a judge make decisions on residence?

One of the most common complaints we get from clients (especially those who lose in residence applications) is 'how can the judge know what is best for my children when he hasn't even met them?'. Of course this is true; a judge can only listen to what is said in court. That is why the welfare report is so important to the court, and why generally so much weight is attached to it, because the family court adviser is the person who represents the court, meets the children and their parents, and sees where they live first-hand. Whichever way a welfare report goes, whether it is in your favour or not, it is worth remembering that while reports can always be challenged, a strong recommendation is rarely ignored by the court. Once the report is available, it is worth taking your legal adviser's advice as to how strong your case is in the light of it, and thinking about whether you are sure you want to proceed if it has gone against you.

Both the family court adviser and the judge must, when making any recommendations or decisions about residence or contact, take into account certain things, which together are known as the 'welfare checklist'. These things include:

- The wishes and feelings of the child in the light of his age and understanding.

- The child's educational, physical and emotional needs.

- The likely effect on the child of any change in circumstances.

- The child's age, sex, and background and any relevant characteristics.

- Any harm the child has suffered or is at risk of suffering.

- How capable the parents are of meeting the child's needs.

No one of these individual items is any more important than another. What is crucial is that the overall decision is, in the judge's view, in the best interests of the child when taking all the above factors into account.

Of course there are many other matters that a judge will also take into account when making a decision on residence. These include how willing each parent would be to promote contact with the other, how capable each parent is of speaking to the children about the other in a positive way, and how strong the children's bond is with each of the parents. A judge will also want to know about a parent's working arrangements, and whether childminding would be needed if a child were to live with him or her, where the children go to school, where their hobbies and friends are, and whether a Residence Order would affect any or all of these routines. It is also the case that a court will always be reluctant to make a Residence Order that would mean a child would move from the place in which he or she is used to living, unless there are very strong reasons for this being in the child's best interests.

If my child says that she wants to live with me, then won't that be enough for the court to decide that this should happen?

Although the court must take into account the wishes of a child, the amount of weight that is placed on them will vary hugely according to the individual circumstances of the case, how old the child is and how clear her views are. The views of a child of 13 who says she wants to live somewhere are likely to be given far more weight than a child of four who says the same thing. The courts are also aware that children often say one thing to one parent and another to the other parent, in trying to please them both.

It is the role of the family court adviser to see whether the child is old enough to have clear views, or whether the child herself is confused about what should happen. The courts are also very reluctant to place on a child the burden of deciding which parent they would rather be with, as no child should be given such a big responsibility. Although their views will certainly be listened to and represented in court, the judge will use them as just one factor in deciding the best outcome for the child in the long term.

If the decision goes against me, can I make a fresh application for residence in the future?

Clients often ask at the end of residence hearings whether they will be able to make another residence application in the future. In theory the answer is yes, though in truth the courts are reluctant to rehear residence applications unless you are able to show a significant change in circumstances so that it is justified. One of the main aims of the courts is to give children who have experienced marital break-up some stability, so that at least they know where they stand and that their futures are not hanging in the balance. For this reason you will need to discuss carefully with your legal advisers whether or not applying to change residence once an order has been made is likely to achieve anything in reality.

Would it be possible for us to have a Joint Residence Order?

Again, in theory it is possible for the courts to make a Joint Residence Order where the children's living arrangements are divided between both parents. For example, the children could spend three nights with one parent and four with the other, or spend alternate weeks between the two. I was even involved in one very unusual case where a young child stayed in the home on a permanent basis and it was the mother and father who took turns in living there with her.

However, having said that all those orders are possible, I must stress that Joint Residence Orders are extremely unusual nowadays and are only made in exceptional circumstances. They certainly won't be made where the two parents do not get on with each other. Unless the parents can show that they have a strong ability to communicate with each other, and can discuss matters that would affect the child, a court will not even consider making an order for joint residence. The irony of it is that if two parents are still able to get on as well as this, they are unlikely to need any involvement by the court at all. Added to that is the fact that, unless two parents live very close to each other, then a Joint Residence Order is likely to cause problems in the child getting to school or nursery easily from two separate addresses.

Perhaps the most important factor against Joint Residence Orders, though, is that children should have a stable and secure base, and feel that they know where their home is, as living in two separate places can be confusing for them. Many parents who come expecting the court to grant a Joint Residence Order find this is not appropriate in their case, but that they can still enjoy a regular relationship with the children through having weekly or fortnightly contact with them.

ISSUES OVER CONTACT

Much of the procedure involved in sorting out contact disputes is the same as it is for residence. If you and your ex cannot agree on how much contact the absent parent should have, than one of you will have to fill in an application form asking the court for an order for 'defined contact'.

This just means that you will have an official document from the court that says when and how often contact between the children and the absent parent should be. You will each file statements, exactly as for the residence procedure, and the family court adviser will have to file a report on what in her view the best way forward should be.

Many parents are surprised (and often upset) to learn that the general rule is that wherever possible a child should have contact with both of his parents. There is a vast range of different reasons why people are reluctant to allow their children to have contact with their ex husband or wife, but there have to be very strong factors showing why contact is *not* in the best interests of a child for a court to say that there should be no contact at all.

The sorts of cases where the court might decide to order no contact are where there has been serious domestic violence between the parents, where a child has been abused, or sometimes where the mother (or indeed father) is so frightened or upset at the thought of contact that she could not cope with it, and that this would result in having an effect on how well she was able to parent the child.

These can become quite complicated arguments, and the scope of this book is not wide enough to cover all the possible scenarios in a contact application. The important point for any court is that the interest of the child is more important than anything, not the wishes and feelings of the parents involved. The matters that the court will consider are the same as for the welfare checklist outlined under the Residence Orders heading (pages 112–113).

In preparing this chapter we asked a family court adviser what advice she would give to clients caught up in a contact dispute, and this is a summary of what she said:

'The general problem is that people expect a solution very quickly. They want contact and they want it immediately. The difficulty with that is that the parent on the other side is often not ready or able to think about contact to begin with.

People can forget that divorce is in some ways like a bereavement. During a divorce it is normal to go through a number of different feelings such as disbelief, anger and feeling traumatised before you get back into gear again and are able to think about routines and getting back to normal. It is easy to forget that, when someone has been through a divorce and has totally lost all trust in their ex, it can sometimes be asking a lot to expect them to trust the same person with the most precious thing in their life… the children.

My advice is that when this happens you have to be patient, and you have to try to rebuild that trust and get some credit back. Take it step by step and don't try to rush things. You need to rebuild a totally new relationship with your ex from scratch… You can't stay in the rut of being the 'ex-husband' or the 'ex-wife' forever, but wounds do not heal overnight. It is important to try and learn to respect your ex again rather than criticise all the time. You cannot expect your children to respect the other parent if you find this impossible yourself. The hardest clients I have are those people who simply cannot move on with their lives, and just rerun the same tune time after time.

My overall advice is to try and agree things with your ex wherever this is possible, even though this means compromising sometimes. This is almost always easier than going through the court process. Sometimes though, where negotiation or counselling or mediation just haven't worked, the court is able to kick-start the whole contact issue again and matters can end up being resolved in the long term.

If you can't avoid the court process, I would remind any parent that children can hear and pick up on a lot of things that are said. They should not be used as messengers between parents, and you should use your energy in reassuring them that both parents love them, rather than just criticising the other parent all the time. In my experience there are very few parents who have absolutely nothing to add to a child's life and that is worth remembering.

Whether you like your ex or not, the child has a right to know who both biological parents are because this helps her form her own sense of identity. A child who does not know her father is likely to think that he is either something terrible, and much worse than he actually is, which will affect her own self-esteem, or that he is a knight in shining armour who one day will come to the rescue. Neither of these fantasies will do any good in the long run. It is almost always better for a child to know her real parents for what they are, warts and all.

At the end of the day the whole issue over contact is about what is best for the children, not for the parents.'

There is no getting away from the fact that proceedings involving the children can be extremely hard and can produce many different emotions, such as insecurity, frustration and protective feelings, but it is crucial to remember that both the parents and the court should have at the front of their minds what is the best result in the long run for the children involved.

What happens if my ex and I can't reach any agreement over contact?

If you find it impossible to reach any contact agreement, then you will have to ask the courts to decide for you by one of you issuing a contact application. The process will then start that leads to a Final Hearing when the final decision on contact is made.

During these contact proceedings there is generally at least one hearing known as a 'directions hearing' where the court decides what steps need to be taken (e.g. the filing of documents, or periods of contact which the family courts adviser can observe) prior to a Final Hearing. It is worth remembering that these short hearings are also opportunities to put forward proposals to the other side through your legal advisers, and sometimes if the family courts adviser is present at court he might also be prepared to help you in having a discussion with your ex as to a possible agreement. If you feel this might help in your case, then it is always worth suggesting as a way forward.

Where no agreement is possible, then you have to move to a final hearing, which is similar to the format of a residence hearing, at the end of which the judge will make a final decision.

Will the children have to come to the Final Hearing?

As a general rule, no. It is very unusual for children to attend at court over issues of contact, or indeed residence. Occasionally a judge will suggest that a child should come and be able to speak directly (usually in private) with the judge, but this is not common.

What will a Contact Order say?

A judge can order as much or as little contact as he thinks is appropriate in a case. Contact could be as little as one hour of supervised contact a month in extreme circumstances, or as much as every weekend and half the school holidays in others. In fact it is quite common for an absent parent to be given contact every alternate weekend and half the school holidays, so do not be surprised if this is something that is suggested to you.

What are the different types of contact that a judge can order?

In any contact dispute you will hear the terms 'direct contact' and 'indirect contact' being used.

Direct contact means that a parent will see the children face to face, and is the most common type of contact. It also includes contact by telephone. Direct contact is generally unsupervised, where a parent can simply see the children either at home or somewhere else, with no one else having to be present to supervise it. Supervised contact can be ordered in situations where the child's welfare may be in question, or when there has been a long gap since the child last saw the parent and the court wishes to know how the child will cope with contact restarting. If the court thinks that supervision is needed, this can be done by either a friend or relative, the family court adviser, or even social services if this is thought appropriate.

Indirect contact is where the child and parent do not meet face to face but keep in contact through letters, cards and presents. Indirect contact can often be used as a first step to re-establishing contact in a situation where it has not happened for some time.

Of course a court order can include both direct and indirect contact, depending on the circumstances in the case. A Contact Order can also be highly specific as to the frequency and duration of contact, or very vague, where it is expected that the parents can make their own arrangements following the court hearing. A court order can also specify that certain people should not be allowed to be present during contact times if this is considered necessary by the court hearing the case.

PROHIBITED STEPS ORDERS

A Prohibited Steps Order is available to stop a parent doing something they would normally be allowed to do as someone with parental responsibility for the child. An example where a Prohibited Steps Order might be appropriate is where one parent is prohibited from taking a child abroad without leave of the court.

SPECIFIC ISSUE ORDERS

These orders are designed to decide any issue that could normally be decided by a person who had parental responsibility over a child. The sorts of things that could be covered by a Specific Issue Order are where a child should go to school or whether or not they can go on a specific holiday.

What can I do to help my children cope with the divorce process?

There is no magic answer to this question as every divorce is different, as is every child, and children will react to their parents splitting up in a vast number of different ways.

However, you can almost certainly help by allowing your children to talk to you or someone else about the situation if they feel comfortable doing so. You can explain what is happening in a way that they are likely to be able to understand and cope with. Wherever possible you should try and remain positive about your ex, reassuring the children that they are loved by both parents. It is important (though not always easy) to try and keep any arguments or disputes away from the children as they are bound to be upset to see their parents in conflict with each other.

You should also try as much as possible to remember that any decisions about the children should be made with their best interests in mind. A person who in your view is a bad husband can still be a good father, and it is sometimes easy to make decisions because of the way you feel rather than what would be best for the children in the long term.

There are several simple leaflets and publications written specifically for children about separation and divorce, and some of these can often be found in the public areas of the county court. A little booklet called *My Family's Splitting Up*, which includes both personal stories and explanations of the process, can be obtained free of charge by writing to Freepost, PO Box 2001, Burgess Hill, West Sussex RH15 8BR.

CHAPTER 9

DOMESTIC VIOLENCE, INJUNCTIONS AND OCCUPATION ORDERS

DOMESTIC VIOLENCE

Domestic violence can take many forms, and is much more common than most people realise. It can involve threats, assaults, and sexual or emotional abuse. It almost always consists of aggressive and controlling behaviour. Sadly, one of the many results of domestic violence is that the victim is often too afraid to do anything about it until matters have become desperate. Some victims put up with domestic violence for years before they manage to summon up the courage to tell anyone about it.

All too often outsiders hearing tales about violence in someone else's marriage say: 'I wouldn't put up with that if it happened to me. I would just leave.' But in truth it is often a lot harder to escape the situation than people think. In writing this chapter we make no value judgements at all; all we can do is give you as much information as possible about the organisations that are able to offer help to victims of domestic violence, and the legal steps that you can take in order to protect yourself from it.

It may be that you are reading this chapter having suffered at the hands of an abusive partner or husband and have not yet been able to do anything about it. If there is one piece of advice that we would like to offer, it is to talk to someone about what you are going through. You should also know that however badly you have suffered, and whatever your situation, you are not alone. Many of the people we speak to who have experienced some form of domestic violence within their relationship feel embarrassed or ashamed even to be talking about it. They often feel that they must be at least partly to blame for the violence they have suffered and that no one could possibly understand why they have put up with it. Victims of domestic violence also frequently feel isolated and alone. All these feelings are extremely common and if any of them apply to you then you are not at all unusual.

What we can say is that however difficult you feel it might be to confide in someone about your situation, there are now many organisations out there that have been set up specifically to offer support and advice to people like you. The people who work for them (many of them volunteers), will be used to hearing all kinds of stories, and are able to listen sympathetically and offer practical help rather than making judgements about the people who call them.

In writing this chapter I made a call to the Women's Aid National 24-hour Domestic Violence Helpline (08457 023468), where I spoke to a worker by the name of Shirley who told me exactly what the helpline aims to do. Shirley explained that its purpose is two-fold, in that it offers a counselling service over the telephone but it can also put callers in touch with agencies and refuges in their local area. Women's Aid runs more than 300 refuges all over the country, but there are also refuges run by other agencies, so it is worth ringing one of the domestic violence helplines to find out where the closest one is to where you live. A refuge can offer safe temporary accommodation in times of crisis, as well as advice and support to help you decide what steps to take next.

Some refuges are described as Family Crisis Centres, offering not only advice and accommodation for both women and children escaping domestic violence, but also programmes designed to help the perpetrators of violence deal with the problem and the issues that surround it. These programmes can be accessed either by self-referral, where a perpetrator asks for help himself, or through another agency such as the probation service where the criminal justice system may have become involved. Of course these programmes cannot guarantee a hundred per cent success rate in putting an end to domestic violence, but they can often be a first step for a perpetrator in dealing with the beliefs and values they have surrounding issues of domestic violence.

I asked Shirley what her advice would be to anyone reading these pages who is in a situation of domestic violence. She said that the most important things to remember were:

- to make yourself safe

- to make sure that your children are safe

- to know that you are not alone in what you are suffering

- to know that there is nothing to feel ashamed or embarrassed about; domestic violence is not the victim's fault

Even if you are in a situation where you find yourself unable to leave, it can still be enormously helpful to talk to someone who is used to hearing about domestic violence. All the helplines offer a completely confidential service, and so if nothing else they can be used to access a sympathetic ear trained to listen to your call without divulging what has been said. In addition to the Women's Aid Helpline, you should also know about an organisation called Refuge which operates a 24-hour national crisis line on 08705 995 443. Other useful contact details are given at the end of this book.

The legal position

If you do decide to take legal action in order to protect yourself against domestic violence or harassment there are basically two types of help that you can apply for through the courts. The first is an order designed to stop your spouse from threatening, harassing or assaulting you in any way. This type of order can be known as either an injunction or a Non-molestation Order. The second type of help is to do with ensuring you have somewhere safe to live, usually by excluding your spouse from your home so you can live there free from the fear of aggressive or violent behaviour. This is known as an Occupation Order.

It is still the case that most situations of domestic violence involve men being violent towards women, so for the sake of simplicity the examples in this chapter refer to the wife as victim. Of course men too are sometimes victims of domestic violence, so it is important to note that all the advice in this chapter applies equally to both sexes.

NON-MOLESTATION ORDERS

You can ask the court to make a Non-molestation Order in any situation where you have suffered from violence, threats or harassment. If you are in this situation and feel that you need some protection from the courts, it is vital that you speak to a solicitor about it immediately. A court will be far more reluctant to grant you an order if you have stayed within the home for a long time following the abusive behaviour. Your solicitor will help you fill in a form explaining the type of order you are asking for and giving brief reasons for the application. You will also have to file a statement (or affidavit) which sets out exactly what has happened to make you apply for such an order. Before any order is made you will have to attend court for the judge to decide whether or not he thinks a Non-molestation Order is needed in your case.

Do I have to tell my husband about the application? If he finds out he'll go mad!

It is often the case that when a person has been living with aggressive or violent behaviour, she feels that applying for an injunction from the court would only make things worse once her partner finds out about it. In these situations it is possible to ask the court to make what is known as an 'ex parte' order. This means that the court can make an injunction order without the husband knowing about it beforehand.

A court will only do this in certain circumstances, for example if the judge thinks that the situation is urgent and that you or the children might suffer harm if the order is not made straight away. He might also make an ex parte order if your spouse is deliberately making sure that he is never available to receive the court papers (what lawyers term 'avoiding service'). For a court to make an ex parte order you would still need to attend court with your solicitor but your spouse would not be present or know that the matter was being heard in court.

Although ex parte orders can be extremely useful in crisis situations, they will generally only be made to last for a short time (often seven days), after which a further court hearing will be listed, known as the 'return date'. By this date your husband will have received the papers in the case and will have an opportunity to attend court and argue that an injunction is not necessary should he choose to do so. It will then be up to the court to decide, having heard from both people, whether or not a Non-molestation Order is needed in your particular case.

What will the Non-molestation Order say?

A Non-molestation Order will direct that your husband refrains from harassing, threatening or assaulting you, and will also order that he does not try to do any of these things through someone else, for example by sending friends round to issue threats on his behalf. In some situations (especially those where the court finds that there has been violence involved), the court will attach a 'power of arrest' to the order. This means that if your husband breaks the terms of the order, the police will have the power to arrest him immediately. He will then be taken to court again so that a judge can decide whether the terms of the order have been broken, and if so what type of punishment is appropriate.

What happens if the judge finds that my husband has broken the terms of the order?

If your husband is arrested through the power of arrest on your injunction, then he will be taken to court automatically within 24 hours of the time of his arrest and both you and your husband will have the opportunity to tell the court your version of events. In cases where there is no power of arrest, and your husband breaks the terms of the injunction, then you yourself can bring what are known as 'committal proceedings' against him with the help of your solicitor. This means that you will tell the court, through your solicitor and a document headed 'Notice to Show Cause' that the terms of the injunction have been broken. Your husband can either admit that he has in fact broken the order, or he can choose to deny the allegations. If he denies what you are saying, then you will have to go to court for a hearing so that the judge can hear both sides of the story and decide which of you he thinks is telling the truth.

If the judge comes to the conclusion that the terms of the order have been broken, then your husband can be punished in several ways. In the most serious cases, a judge can order that he serves a period of immediate imprisonment. He can also order what is known as a 'suspended sentence'. This means that the judge has given your husband a sentence of (for example) two months, but it will not have to be served immediately. If your husband leaves court and does not commit any further breaches of the injunction, he may never have to serve the sentence: but if he breaches the order again, the judge will usually make him serve the suspended sentence as well as ordering a further punishment for the second breach of the order. The judge can also decide to punish your husband by fining him.

What is an undertaking?

An undertaking is a promise that is made to the court either to do certain things, or to refrain from doing them. When a wife applies to court for an injunction against her husband, the husband's solicitor might sometimes suggest that he give an 'undertaking' rather than having to have an injunction made against him. The advantage of an undertaking is that you will not have to go through a court hearing to get one. It might also be an attractive option to the husband because he can offer an undertaking to the court without any 'findings' being made against him.

An undertaking is just as serious as an injunction, and breaking it can lead to exactly the same punishments as those described above. The only real difference is that a court is not able to attach a power of arrest to an undertaking, so if you think this is important in your case, it may be that your solicitor will advise you that an injunction would be more suitable in your situation.

OCCUPATION ORDERS

The other type of order that can offer you protection is known as an Occupation Order. This type of order can be used to determine who should stay in a property and who should leave it. It is very flexible in that it can force someone to leave a property, it can give someone the right to re-enter a property, or it can exclude a person from parts of a property, effectively creating two separate living areas within one house.

In deciding whether or not to make an Occupation Order, a judge will consider several matters. These include:

- the housing needs of both parties and any relevant children

- the financial situation of everyone involved

- the conduct of the parties towards each other and otherwise

- the likely effect of making (or not making) an Occupation Order on the health, safety and well-being of the parties and the children (if any)

If a judge is satisfied that one or more people would suffer 'significant harm' without an order, then the court has a duty to make an Occupation Order. In doing this the judge will carry out an exercise called the 'balance of harm' test. In general terms, this means deciding whether or not an order should be made, given the likely effect (and possible harm) that would result to each person involved.

Once the judge has thought through the various options, he has to decide which of those options would be likely to cause least harm. The judge will be particularly concerned with the welfare of any children involved, and will put their needs and well-being very high on his list of priorities. Where it is clear which parent is going to be living and caring for the children, it is often the case that the other parent will have to move out of the home where the situation justifies the making of an Occupation Order.

Rachel and Brian

In this case, Rachel and her husband Brian were living together with their two daughters. The marriage had been unhappy for a long time, but recently Brian had resorted to calling Rachel names in front of the children, being extremely verbally aggressive, and leaving rude messages for her all over the house. Although Brian had not been violent towards Rachel he had been extremely emotionally abusive towards her. Rachel became so depressed by the situation that she was prescribed anti-depressants and had to take some time off work. Her doctor diagnosed her as suffering from severe stress caused by the atmosphere at home. In addition Rachel's elder daughter began having problems at school, often becoming very tearful and sometimes even refusing to eat because she was finding the whole situation at home so difficult to handle.

Although Rachel had already filed divorce papers, Brian had made it clear that he was not prepared to leave the house and intended to stay there however bad the atmosphere was. Rachel's solicitor advised her to apply to the court for an Occupation Order that would require Brian to leave the house so that Rachel could stay there with her two daughters.

At court, the judge read the statements by both Rachel and Brian, read a letter from Rachel's doctor saying how much stress she was under, and also heard both Rachel and Brian give evidence about the situation. The judge also found out that Brian would be able to stay at his mother's house on a temporary basis. He decided in this case that he *should* make an Occupation Order, which would require Brian to leave the property. The reason for this was that in the circumstances he thought that Rachel would suffer more harm if the two of them stayed in the house together than Brian would if he was asked to leave. He was also concerned that Rachel's daughter appeared to be suffering from the stress as well. This is a very simplified example of how the balance of harm test can work when a judge is asked to make an Occupation Order.

Mary and Simon

According to Mary, her husband had been violent to her on several occasions, whereas Simon denied ever having been violent and said that Mary had a serious drinking problem and often lost her temper herself. On one occasion they had rowed so badly that Simon had thrown Mary out of the house, and she had been staying with several different friends since. Their two sons had remained at home with their father.

As in the previous case, Mary had applied to the court for an Occupation Order, saying that the house was jointly owned and she should have the right to return to it. The judge found this case very difficult, because on one hand it did not seem right that Mary should not be able to enter her home because of Simon's actions, but on the other hand he did not think it was practical for them to be living under the same roof. The reason for this was that the house was a small one with only two bedrooms. Whichever of them was telling the truth about the relationship, it was certainly clear that Mary and Simon were arguing all the time and that it could not be a good environment for the children to be living in. The judge also found out that if he ordered that Mary could move back in to the house, the only place she would have to sleep was in the bedroom with her two sons, and he didn't think that this was a very satisfactory arrangement.

Another important point in this case was that the parents were still arguing as to which of them the boys should live with, and no decision had yet been made about that by the court.

The judge decided in this case *not* to make an Occupation Order. Even though he felt that Mary should have the right to return to the home, he also felt that the boys would suffer if they were put back in a situation where their parents were living together in such a small house. On balance, the judge felt that the boys would suffer more harm as a result of an order being made allowing Mary back into the house than Mary would suffer without one. He decided that Mary could manage for a short time by staying with her friends, and that the issue of who should live in the house would be sorted out once a final decision had been made about which parent the boys should live with.

Graham and Linda

A significant difference in this case is that this couple lived in a large house, with four bedrooms and two bathrooms. In their case the judge thought that an Occupation Order should be made, but did it in such a way that they both had access to separate parts of the property. Graham was ordered to stay out of Linda's part of the house, and she was ordered to stay out of the part that Graham would be using. Although, of course, this type of living arrangement is not an ideal one, it can at least offer a temporary solution to this type of problem. In this case both Linda and Graham still had somewhere to live until the finances were finally resolved, but also came into contact with each other as little as possible.

If an Occupation Order is made against my husband, does that mean that I own the property outright?

No it doesn't. It is important to mention that even where an Occupation Order is made that excludes someone from their home, this has no effect on their rights to it financially. The house will not become the sole property of the wife just because the husband is asked to leave it. All matters to do with ownership and finances are considered completely separately from Occupation Orders, and the factors that are taken into account when deciding who should keep the house are looked at on pages 83–87.

How long do Non-molestation and Occupation Orders last?

There is no set time period for the duration of these orders; this is something that is up to the judge. A typical time period for a Non-molestation Order is often six months to begin with. If the order is breached in any way, then it is usual for a judge to extend the order so that the protection lasts for a longer period.

Stopping domestic violence

If you read the stories told by Alicia (page 159) and Louise (page 162), you can see that they shared many of the same feelings of guilt, embarrassment, shame and isolation despite their different circumstances. It may well be that if you know someone trapped in a violent relationship they are also experiencing emotions such as these. Unfortunately, no one can force another person to leave a violent relationship if they are not ready to do it themselves, but it is important to know that there is help available, and being aware of the organisations and legal remedies that exist should go some way towards reassuring people experiencing domestic violence that it does not have to go on forever.

CHAPTER 10

LIVING TOGETHER

Although this book is aimed at married people either thinking about or going through the divorce process, there will be those reading it as a result of having to deal with separation from a partner to whom they have never been married. It is important to know that, while separating from a partner can be just as upsetting and traumatic as divorcing a husband or wife, the laws that govern how your separation is dealt with are in some respects completely different from those relating to divorce.

The first and most obvious point is that because you and your ex-partner have never been married, you will not have to go through the process of divorce at all. Once the decision has been made to separate you are free to go your own ways without the law having to become involved at any stage. Having said that, you may still find that there are issues between you concerning finances, property or your children, and you may wonder how you should go about resolving these matters.

These few pages do not in any way set out to answer all your questions in relation to separation, but there are a few factors that it might be worth pointing out to those of you in that situation. For example, if you find that you and your ex-partner are in disagreement about your children, then much of the procedure to do with sorting out issues of contact and residence will be the same as for married couples who are separating. The one major difference is to do with parental responsibility.

What is parental responsibility?

Parental responsibility is the term to describe all the rights, duties, powers and responsibilities that a parent has towards his or her children. In simple terms this means things like deciding where a child should go to school. A mother will always have automatic parental responsibility in respect of her children. A father, however, does not have automatic parental responsibility. A father will have parental responsibility if he was married to the child's mother at the time the child in question was born, and will usually obtain parental responsibility if he marries the child's mother at a later date.

However, if the father has never been married to the child's mother, then he has no automatic right to parental responsibility. He can gain it either by agreement with the child's mother, or by order of the court. If the mother does not agree to the father having parental responsibility, then he will have to apply through the court system for it to be granted. In most situations such as these, the court will agree to granting a father parental responsibility unless he has acted in such a way that the court thinks it would not be in the child's interests for this to happen.

If we have not been married but have children together, what will happen if we can't agree who the children should live with, or how much contact there should be?

Apart from the point on parental responsibility, the way in which disputes on both contact and residence are decided is broadly the same for all sets of parents, whether they have been married to each other or not.

Where an agreement is not reached between the parents about where the children should live or how much contact there should be with the absent parent, an application can be made to the court by either mother or father in exactly the same way as for married parents. The court will use the same criteria (always with the welfare of the children as the most important concern) in making any decision in respect of the children. These are explained fully in Chapter 8.

The financial situation

The biggest difference between married couples who divorce and unmarried couples who separate after co-habiting is in relation to their financial positions. Chapter 7 sets out the way in which the finances are dealt with for married couples following a divorce petition being issued. However, we should make it clear that almost none of the information contained within that chapter will have any relevance to an unmarried couple who decide to separate.

Many people still seem to think that if you live with someone for a certain length of time (six months is commonly suggested) that you begin to have rights of ownership over the other person's property. We cannot stress strongly enough that this is simply not true. There is no law in existence in England and Wales that allows you to have a claim on someone's property simply by living with them (regardless of however many children you might have together), even if the relationship has lasted for 20 years!

The starting point for an unmarried couple who are separating is that you keep what is in your name and your ex-partner keeps what is in his. Whereas most things owned by either husband or wife will be known as a 'matrimonial asset' and be available for the court to give to either party following a divorce, the same is absolutely not the case for partners who have not been married. It therefore becomes much more relevant to know, for example, whose name the house is in. In simple terms, if you are not a legal owner of the property, then you may well not have a claim to any part of it.

Is it the case that if my name is not on the title deeds then it is impossible for me to claim any financial interest in the house I have lived in?

Not entirely, as there is a way in which you may be able to claim an interest in a house that you do not officially own. You should be warned however that this is a tricky area of the law (even to most lawyers!), and entirely separate from the rules mentioned about property for married couples on pages 83–87. Let's use an example.

If John and Sarah live together in a property that John bought in his own name, then if they decide to separate the law says that John owns the property outright and Sarah has no right to either the property or any money from it. However, Sarah might argue that she has lived in the house for the last eight years, and that she has put a lot of money into improving the property. Sarah might quite understandably feel that she should receive some money from the property when the relationship comes to an end.

In this type of situation Sarah would have to make an application to the court, asking it to make a declaration that she should have something called a 'beneficial interest' in the property. This would mean that the court would decide that she should have some financial interest in the house even though she is not its legal owner.

This is not an easy thing for Sarah to achieve and, in order to have a chance of doing so, she has to show firstly that there was some sort of agreement between her and John that she would have a financial interest in the property, and secondly that she has both relied on that agreement and spent money on the property (or otherwise 'acted to her detriment') because of it. It would not be enough for Sarah to say that she had contributed to the property by, for example, staying at home to look after the children (as it would be if she had been married).

As I explained earlier, this area of the law is not straightforward, and if you are in a situation where you feel you have a claim on a property that you do not legally own, then you are strongly advised to take legal advice about the strength of your case.

You will need to find out whether or not you can prove that you have a beneficial interest in the property and your solicitor should be able to give you advice as to whether the matter is worth taking to court. Be aware that if the case does get as far as the courtroom, and the judge thinks you should be entitled to a share of the property, he will still have quite a lot of discretion as to how big your share should be. He is certainly not obliged to order that you should receive 50 per cent of the property's value, and he could decide that your share is much less than that. It is often very difficult for a solicitor to give an accurate prediction of how the case will finish up if it goes to court, so if a decent offer is made to you from the other side at any stage of the negotiations it is worth thinking about it seriously, as going to court in this area of law can be a risky business and very high in legal costs.

Can I claim maintenance from my ex-partner?

If you have not been married, then you do not have a right to claim the equivalent of the 'spousal maintenance' that you would be able to claim had you been married. You only 'earn' the right to be financially maintained by a partner if you have been married to them, you do not earn this right simply by living together, however unfair this may seem. In relation to the children, however, your rights are exactly the same as if you had been married in that you are entitled to make a claim for Child Support through the Child Support Agency, and the rules regarding how much your ex will have to pay are the same regardless of whether you were once married or not. There is more information on claiming through the Child Support Agency on pages 143–144.

Can I still ask the court for an injunction or an Occupation Order against my ex-partner if we have not been married?

Yes you can. Issues of domestic violence, Occupation Orders and Non-molestation Orders (or injunctions) are discussed fully in Chapter 9.

Since the introduction of Part IV of the Family Law Act in 1996, unmarried couples are now able to benefit from the same protection from the courts as can those people who have been married. This part of the law describes people who have lived together as husband and wife as 'associated persons' for the purposes of these rules and you are therefore able to apply for the same forms of protection that are available to married couples. If you are in need of this type of protection then you will find the procedure set out fully in Chapter 9.

Conclusions

It is not within the scope of this book to go through all the various scenarios that might apply to unmarried couples who live together, but you will find that much of the information on children, mediation, and domestic violence is still relevant even if you have not been married to your partner. As already explained, the biggest difference between married and co-habiting couples who separate can be found in the way the finances are dealt with. In this area, marriage still brings with it many more rights and responsibilities than co-habitation does. Don't forget, though, that many solicitors offer a free first consultation, so you will lose nothing by approaching a solicitor to find out exactly how you stand financially following the break-up of your relationship with your partner.

CHAPTER 11

NOTES ON STATE BENEFITS AND CHILD SUPPORT

A guide to state benefits

Most people who go through the divorce process will also experience a change in their financial circumstances. If you find yourself under pressure to make ends meet, it may well be worth checking to see if you are eligible for any help through the state benefits system.

There are several different benefits that are potentially available to divorced people who are struggling financially (whether in the short- or long-term), many of which go unclaimed simply because people do not realise that they are entitled to them. The following pages give a brief explanation of the benefits that are available and who would be likely to qualify for them. We should stress that this is a rough guide only, so if you are in any doubt as to whether you qualify for a particular benefit, we suggest that you make an appointment at your local benefits office where someone will be able to look at your individual circumstances.

Jobseeker's Allowance

Jobseeker's Allowance (JSA) is available to people over 18 and under 65 (for men) or under 60 (for women). To qualify, you must be capable of working, and either unemployed or working less than 16 hours per week. If for any reason it has been decided that you are incapable of working then you should claim Incapacity Benefit (see pages 142–143) rather than JSA. You must also be actively looking for work to receive Jobseeker's Allowance, which means that you must be 'willing and able' to take up work 'immediately'.

The amount of JSA you receive is likely to be reduced if you have savings of over £3000 (£6000 if you are over 60). If you have over £8000 in savings then you are unlikely to qualify for JSA at all. You should also note that you cannot receive both JSA and Income Support (see below) at the same time. If you find that you do qualify for JSA, then you might also be entitled to extra benefits, such as free milk and vitamins for pregnant women and children under five, and you may also qualify for help with your housing costs. To claim JSA you must apply through your local Jobcentre.

Income Support

Income Support is a benefit for people on a low income with savings of less than £8000. You will not be entitled to claim Income Support if you have signed on at the Jobcentre and declared yourself available for work, in which case you should be claiming Jobseeker's Allowance.

In order to claim Income Support you must be over 16, on a low income and either not working or working less than 16 hours per week. There are several categories of people who qualify for Income Support, and these include lone parents (either not working or working less than 16 hours per week). If you are working over 16 hours per week, you may still qualify for the Child Tax Credit (see page 139) or the Working Tax Credit (see page 140). Those who do qualify for Income Support are also entitled to free milk and vitamins, and you may also qualify for help with housing costs.

Other benefits

If you receive either Jobseeker's Allowance or Income Support, you will also be entitled to help with your health costs. These include:

- free NHS prescriptions

- free NHS dental treatment

- free NHS sight tests

- help towards travel costs to and from hospital for NHS treatment

Child Benefit

You are entitled to claim Child Benefit if you have children living with you, regardless of your income. The child must be either under 16, under 19 if still in full-time education, or under 18 if they are registered at the careers office for work or work-related training. It is worth remembering that only one person can claim Child Benefit in respect of each child. Generally the person claiming the benefit will be the person the child is living with. If the child has come to live with you, and someone else (e.g. the other parent) is still receiving the Child Benefit, you can ask the Child Benefit Centre to pay the benefit to you instead. They can be contacted on 08701 555540.

Working Families' Tax Credit

The Working Families' Tax Credit ceased to exist as from April 2003. It was replaced by the Child Tax Credit and the Working Tax Credit. It is important to note that for both these new credits, once you have separated from your spouse you can claim based on your individual circumstances and your spouse's income will be ignored. If you are still living with your spouse and living together as a married couple then it is your joint income that will be taken into account.

Child Tax Credit

Child Tax Credit (CTC) is available only to families or individuals with children. You do not have to be working to be eligible for CTC. It can be paid up to 1 September following the child's 16th birthday, or in respect of a person between the ages of 16 and 18 if they are still in full-time education. CTC is paid in addition to Child Benefit and the Working Tax Credit.

The amount of CTC that you will receive will depend on the level of your income, but some level of support is generally available to households where the yearly income is less than £58,000. If you are in receipt of either Income Support or income-based Jobseeker's Allowance, then you will be entitled to receive the maximum amount of CTC, which in April 2003 was £38 per week for one child, £65.70 per week for two children, and £93.30 per week for three children.

Working Tax Credit

Working Tax Credit (WTC) is a payment that tops up the earnings of people on low income. It differs from the old Working Families' Tax Credit in that you do not have to have children to qualify for it. For families that do have children, you can claim WTC in addition to Child Tax Credit.

- If you do have children, you must be working at least 16 hours per week to qualify.

- If you do not have children, you must be over 25 and working at least 30 hours a week to qualify.

You can also claim if you are over 16, working at least 16 hours a week and have a disability that puts you at a disadvantage in getting a job.

We will not go into detail as to the amount you can claim based on different levels of earnings as these figures would be likely to be out of date by the time you come to read this book, but at April 2003 it would be fair to say that you have a potential claim to WTC if your yearly income is less than £15,000. Working Tax Credit will be paid in addition to any Child Tax Credit that you may eligible for.

If you have children you may also be entitled to claim for help towards the cost of childcare. The figures as at April 2003 allow you to claim back up to 70p for every pound that you spend on childcare up to a limit of £135 per week for one child (i.e. a maximum claim of £94.50 per week) or £200 a week for two or more children (a maximum claim of £140 per week).

If you think you might be entitled to WTC, then you can fill in a form from your local benefits office, or by going online at www.inlandrevenue.gov.uk/taxcredits. You can also ring the helpline on 0845 300 3900.

For further information on the various benefits available, you can pick up the relevant leaflets and helpsheets at your local benefits office, or you can ring the Orderline on 0845 9000 604. Alternatively you can obtain them via the internet at www.inlandrevenue.gov.uk.

The Social Fund

The Social Fund is available to help with exceptional expenses that you would have difficulty meeting from your own income. If you are receiving either Income Support or income-based Jobseeker's Allowance, you may be entitled to either a Community Care Grant or a Budgeting Loan.

A Community Care Grant is a sum of money that does not have to be repaid and is discretionary. You must already be receiving either Income Support or Jobseeker's Allowance to claim it. One of the reasons for claiming a Community Care Grant can be 'to ease exceptional pressures on you and your family', which could arise as a result of a recent separation or divorce.

A Budgeting Loan is an interest-free loan of between £30 and £1000, and will be available only if you have already been in receipt of either Income Support or Jobseeker's Allowance for 26 weeks prior to making your application. You must also show that you will be able to repay the loan.

There is a long list of items that will not be covered by either a Community Care Grant or a Budgeting Loan, so it is worth checking to see whether or not your financial need is something that they could cover. However, it is worth knowing that both Community Care Grants and Budgeting Loans can be available to pay advance rent to a landlord other than a local authority. This could be a useful short-term solution if you find yourself in the position of having to find immediate private rented accommodation.

If you are not receiving either Income Support or Jobseeker's Allowance then you may still qualify for a Crisis Loan. This is an interest-free loan of up to £1000 designed to help you in an emergency where a Crisis Loan would be the only way of preventing damage or risk to the health of you or a member of your family. A Crisis Loan will have to be repaid so you will need to show that you are able to repay the loan before it can be awarded.

If you think you may be eligible for any of the grants or loans from the Social Fund, then it is worth making further inquiries from your local benefits office.

Housing Benefit and Council Tax Benefit

Both these benefits are paid by local councils to help people on a low income pay their rent and Council Tax. If you are applying for either Income Support or Jobseeker's Allowance, then you can claim for both Housing Benefit and Council Tax Benefit at the same time, and the forms to do this will be provided to you along with your main claim forms. If you are not claiming either Income Support or Jobseeker's Allowance, you must claim Housing Benefit and Council Tax Benefit direct from your local council.

In brief, Housing Benefit is available to help with meeting the cost of rental charges. It cannot be claimed to meet mortgage payments or to buy a home. Housing Benefit is calculated based on your needs, your income and resources, the amount of rent that you pay, who you live with and what would be considered a reasonable rent for your particular home compared to the local average. Any savings you have over £3000 will reduce the amount of benefit that you can receive, and if you have £16,000 in savings you will not be entitled to claim either of these benefits at all. The rules regarding claims for housing benefit and council tax benefit are fully explained in the guide 'RR2', which is available free from your local benefits office.

Disability Living Allowance

Disability Living Allowance is a benefit for those people who need help with either getting around or with personal care. It is not normally affected by the amount of income or savings that you have. The amount you can claim will depend on the amount and type of help that you need. You can call the Benefits Enquiry Line on 0800 882200 for more information or you can write to Disability Living Allowance, Warbreck House, Warbreck Hill, Blackpool FY2 OYE.

Incapacity Benefit

Incapacity Benefit is paid to people who are incapable of work. It is not affected by whether or not you are employed or by how much money you have in the way of savings or income. There are three rates of Incapacity Benefit, and the rate that you receive will depend on the length of time that you have been entitled to receive it. To qualify, you must be at least 16 and below 65 for a man and 60 for a woman. The rules surrounding who may apply for Incapacity Benefit and under what circumstances you will be treated as incapable of work are quite involved, and so we will not attempt to set them out here. If you think you may be eligible for this benefit then you should contact your local benefits office for more details.

Child Support

Child Support differs from the other benefits described above because it is paid by the absent parent rather than by the state.

If you are bringing up children, you are entitled to claim maintenance from the children's other natural parent. A parent is entitled to claim Child Support for any children living with them who are either under 16 or between 16 and 19 and in full-time education. The level of Child Support to be paid is calculated by the Child Support Agency (CSA).

Unless the absent parent is paying an agreed amount of Child Support on a voluntary basis, you will have to apply to the CSA in order for them to work out how much the absent parent should be paying you in respect of the children. The new rules are much simpler than the old ones, in that the CSA now just works out the absent parent's net weekly income, and from this figure will order a payment of 15 per cent for one child, 20 per cent for two children, and 25 per cent for three or more children. If the absent parent has a net weekly income of between £100 and £200 they will pay a reduced rate of Child Support. This will be £5 per week plus a percentage of the income over £100. If the child regularly stays overnight with his or her other parent (for at least an average of one night a week), then the amount of Child Support that you receive will be reduced.

To apply for Child Support or to get more information, you can ring the CSA National Enquiry Line on 08457 133 133. It is important to note that, when you apply for Child Support, you will have to supply the CSA with as much information as you have about the whereabouts of the absent parent. If you do not know where they are, then the CSA will be responsible for trying to trace them through Social Security or Inland Revenue records. If the absent parent still can't be traced, then you must notify the CSA as soon as you find any information that may help them to locate the absent parent's whereabouts.

If an absent parent refuses to pay once the CSA has calculated the right level of child maintenance, then the CSA can deduct the money direct from their earnings and take action against them through the courts if necessary.

CHAPTER 12
PERSONAL STORIES

During the course of writing this book we spoke to many people about their own experiences of the divorce process. Originally we had planned to scatter personal anecdotes throughout the book, to give real examples on all the topics covered in it. The more we spoke to people though, the more we realised that almost everyone had a story to tell that covered several different issues. The other thing they had in common was that they all wished to pass on advice gleaned from their own experiences to others thinking about entering the divorce process. In the end we decided to devote this final chapter to a number of different personal stories, which between them cover many of the topics featured in this book.

All the accounts that follow are true ones. We have told each story exactly the way it was told to us. We asked people about their own experience of divorce, how it had made them feel, and the things they wished they had known earlier. We should also add that the majority of these stories did not come from our own personal clients, so when someone's story says how magnificent the solicitor was, that is no reflection on either of us!

Despite the fact that their individual circumstances varied enormously, some themes reappeared time and time again. Most people felt they had been unjustly treated. The vast majority was surprised at how their ex-husband or ex-wife had behaved during the divorce process, and many stated that they felt stupid and gullible for their own mistakes. They all described periods when they had felt extremely low, miserable and depressed, but few expressed any long-term regrets. In fact not only did the people we spoke to often say they now felt fantastic about the life changes they had made, but they also said that their biggest mistake was not doing anything about the problems in the marriage earlier!

In the following pages, you may or may not find a story that has similarities with your own situation but, at the very least, you may gain some reassurance from knowing that other people have survived what can be a very difficult and painful process, and that most have come out the other side knowing that they made the right decision in the circumstances.

The other theme that came across very strongly however, was how difficult it can be to take the first steps in the divorce process even when it is clear that the marriage is failing. People described going to a solicitor for the first time, or even admitting to problems in the marriage to friends, as being some of the toughest decisions they had ever faced. Many, many people put off making that first move for a long time. If this in any way describes your situation, you can at least take some comfort from the fact that you are not alone in feeling that you can't cope with doing anything about it, that there are thousands of people in exactly your position.

Our first story, in particular, describes one lady who had been desperately unhappy in her marriage for several years. We asked her why she took so long to do anything to resolve the situation.

Anna's story

Why do some people stay in a marriage when it has been unhappy for years? Why have I stayed? It can be something as simple as walking into a shop and not having a wedding ring on. I personally couldn't face knowing there was no one else, and that I was on my own. Loneliness is a massive issue, even though it sounds crazy to want to be with someone who does not make you happy. I have been married 13 years and at least the last five have been horrendous, but in a way sometimes even that can be better than just having to be on your own. There are the other things too, like staying within your comfort zone and not being able to jump out of it.

I have been hammered that far into the ground that I haven't got the mental strength to move on. In order to change this – and for me to actually be spurred into doing something – my health, my job situation and my self-confidence all need to improve. I need good friends, and the confidence that I can do things for myself, but I am not there yet. I also have health problems, and with health problems you somehow feel even more inferior because you are not equal to people any more, and when you are in a bad marriage you end up doing things that compromise your health even further.

Every time he does something bad to me it makes me feel like self-harming, or doing something detrimental to my health, because I don't care any more. Most of the time I just feel like giving up, and the only reason I get up in the mornings is because of my son. If it wasn't for him I don't think I would even be here any more. I am in a big circle that goes round and round and then something else goes wrong; then my health suffers further because of the stress. I know in my heart of hearts that I should leave. Everybody who knows what is going on tells me I should leave, but I don't confide in many people; I am a very private person and to be honest I am ashamed to admit that my marriage has failed. I don't want the stigma of a divorce attached to me. Maybe that is old-fashioned but that is the way I feel.

The truth is that one day things will probably get so bad that I will be forced to go, but I don't know when that time will come, or if I will ever feel strong enough to make that first move myself. I will just have to wait and see how things go.

Caitlin's story

I got divorced five years ago after only being married for two, though we'd been together for longer and had three children.

I have to be honest and say that in terms of the legal part of things, it went pretty smoothly. My solicitor was fantastic. He took over organising everything, and he needed to because I was quite genuinely on the verge of a nervous breakdown. I was suffering from severe depression at the time. I was having counselling, was on medication for stress, and I went through a stage where I self-harmed as well. I was a student with no money and I had three kids to support, all under five. There were days when I just thought there was no point in getting up in the morning, but I knew I had to for the sake of the kids.

We had been separated for a couple of months and had both got into other relationships, and in the end he filed the divorce petition using my adultery as the reason. I didn't like the fact he had done that even though it was true that technically I had been unfaithful. Half of me wanted to deny it and use his own adultery against him, because it didn't seem fair that I should take all the blame when he had done exactly the same thing. I told my solicitor how I felt but he said that in the end if I wanted to get divorced then it was easier just to go along with it and swallow my pride, so that is what I did.

In terms of money he didn't give me a penny. There was hardly anything to split between us. We had a house with only £4000 equity in it and that was about it. What was worse, though, was that for ages he refused to move out of the house, saying that me and the kids would have to get a council house. He said he didn't care if we ended up on the streets. In the end we got the house back, but not before I had spent months of worrying and stressing over it.

I got the money in the house and some of the contents, but he had already taken anything that was of any value, like the microwave, the video and the computer. I could have fought for more, but I didn't have the energy. I was too tired, fed up and low to fight more than I did. I didn't ask for any maintenance and I didn't even go to the CSA. Loads of people kept telling me how stupid I was but I did what I felt I could cope with at the time.

In terms of contact I always said he could see the children when he liked, but after only a few months he seemed to lose interest. He has not seen them now for almost four years. To be honest that upsets me more than anything; the fact that he could just turn his back on the children and pretend that they don't exist. I have heard now that he is remarried, so I suppose he doesn't want his old family to interfere with his new one.

My life has moved on completely. I have married again, I have a fantastic career and earn a lot more than I did when I was with my husband, though all the debts he left me with still affect my credit rating today.

I know it sounds strange after five years, but now I have got over the worst of it, now I have sorted out my own life and moved on, I am planning to go to the CSA later this year. I know he earns reasonable money and I don't see why he should spend his whole life making no contribution to the children's upbringing at all. I am hoping to get a couple of thousand a year from him through the CSA, and I plan to put it to one side so that the children will have something to fall back on when they are older. It will be a huge advantage for them to have that money, and to be honest I will quite enjoy the fact that I have caught up with him after he turned his back on us for so many years. He may have wanted to be rid of me, but in my book turning your back on three children is simply unforgivable.

Stuart's story

I was married for 10 years altogether and it was my wife who filed for divorce after we had agreed that was what we both wanted. It was four years ago now.

She filed on the grounds of unreasonable behaviour but, even though I was expecting the papers, when I got them I felt what she had said was a pack of lies. I was hurt, but I thought if that was the only way we could divorce then that was the way it had to be. In her statement of unreasonable behaviour she said that the marriage had been full of violence and verbal abuse from me. That was just not true.

The first two years were wedded bliss, even though that may sound like a cliché, but then we had our son and she became totally over-possessive. Her parents were also far too involved and I felt pushed out by them. It went downhill from there. In the end we lived two separate lives, and in my view she became completely obsessed with our son. I felt I was only a meal ticket, nothing but a chequebook. There was no meaning left in my role at home.

A combination of things led me to ask for the divorce in the end. For instance she wouldn't support my career, she did not want me to work abroad or in the family business. She wouldn't move anywhere except closer to her parents, who were pulling all the strings. If our son ever did something wrong and I told him off they would always pass comment on it when it was nothing to do with them. All this had gone on for a long time, but then my father died and I just couldn't talk about how I was feeling to my ex. She didn't understand what I was going through and I found myself unable to let my emotions out. We stopped going out or doing things together, or she wouldn't unless our son was with us. We had no friends and no social life. I also had suspicions that she had had an affair with a friend of mine but I could never prove it.

The divorce took over 18 months to go through because the decree absolute could not be completed until the finances were settled. Because of the money in my father's business and the fact that he had died my wife and her legal team assumed I had had a large inheritance, which was not true. They were asking for silly money from me and I just didn't have it. The total assets were only about £45,000 and I ended up walking away with £8500, which was what was left of the money my father had left me. All the rest went to her.

On top of that I had to pay maintenance and I am still paying it. I have to pay it until 2004, a total of five years because by then our daughter will be five and can go to full-time school and my ex-wife can go out to work. However there is a clause to say that if for any reason she can't work she can come back to court to claim more spousal maintenance.

Although I am earning more now, at the time the order was made I was earning about £1500 a month and was paying my ex £750 of it. On top of that I had to make CSA payments. There were some months when I was paying out more than I was earning. I argued with the CSA over it for three years but I got nowhere. I understand that a woman needs money to support the children but I also needed money to live and nobody seemed to understand that. I feel strongly that the court did not listen to what I had to say. It was a very unfair process and is biased towards women. I appreciate there are children involved but I could not afford to live and the court was not interested.

In addition to that, the whole thing took too long, far too long, especially as I had to pay private legal costs and my wife got Legal Aid. I wish I'd have known how much it would cost, how long it would last and what was a reasonable settlement. I didn't get any real answers to those questions until the end of it all. My solicitor made a fairly good guess on the eventual settlement but I wasn't told how much it would cost me in legal fees and I ended up paying £4000. I never expected that.

On the issue of contact the system failed both me and the children. After nearly four years it has not taken my requests to see the children into account, and soon it will be two years since I have seen them. There have been three court orders that I should have some contact with my children but my ex has just ignored them. The family court adviser was on my side and thought I should see the children, and there was even a psychologist involved who reported that my wife treated my son almost like a surrogate partner. It was agreed that my wife should have some counselling to persuade her to restart contact but nothing happened; she just refused to go.

Luckily the family court adviser keeps recommending that I should see my daughter and that is what I am still fighting for. I know that my ex won't even pass on Christmas cards, presents and letters from me. The children have received nothing from me in over two years. Despite the fact there are court orders in my favour, the court has not wished to enforce those orders, and I am still going to court trying desperately to re-establish a relationship with my children.

As far as my ex is concerned this is not about the children any more. She is just bitter. She told me once that she would end up with everything – the house, the money and the love of the children – and I would get nothing, and that is exactly what has happened. Those words will always be embedded in my mind. They haunt me.

At the end of the day, the suffering that the children have gone through because of the divorce has been magnified by her selfishness. I do still believe that she is not all there. My biggest wish would be that I could see the kids again, but I feel that I am not just fighting my ex-wife, I am fighting the system. I am close to giving up because I feel I just can't win. I have done everything by the book, not broken any rules, but it has got me nowhere.

My advice to anyone thinking about a divorce would be to ask yourself whether that is definitely what you want to do. It is extremely painful emotionally and destructive financially. If you can't resolve things try to do as much as you can between yourselves, as amicably as possible, without involving the legal system. Apart from not seeing my children, though, I am much happier now. I have remarried and am very happy with my new wife so I have not given up on the idea of marriage altogether. This time it's the total opposite, it is a partnership, though I know now there are no guarantees in life. Only death and taxes.

Julie's story

It wasn't my divorce itself that was the nightmare, it was what happened with all the stuff around contact. I had four children, two by my first boyfriend and two sons by my ex.

The whole thing was over something that happened one night after we had had some friends over for a few drinks. I'd had a bath and then gone to bed. Our son who was four had climbed into the bed also and later on my ex came to bed. When I woke up a couple of hours later I couldn't believe what I was seeing. My ex was doing indecent things to my 4-year-old right there in front of me, in our bed. I screamed at him and he jumped up and ran out of the room. He put his clothes on and got into his car, driving off like an idiot. He ended up crashing the car that night. What still amazes me is that it seems my son slept through the whole thing.

I have never seen my ex since that day, but the nightmare started when he applied for contact. I told my solicitor and my barrister what had happened and it was all put down in a statement for me. Of course my ex denied everything and said I was making it all up. When it got to court we were supposed to have a hearing so that I could prove what had gone on. All I wanted was to stop him having contact with the kids. I could never trust him again after what I had seen.

The thing was, with there being no medical evidence, the judge said that he wouldn't be able to know one way or the other who was telling the truth. It was awful. I know what I saw but it felt as though no one was really on my side. He kept pushing for contact and, though I didn't want it to happen, the family court adviser thought that I should agree to some contact; letters and cards at first and then some face-to-face contact that was supervised. The whole thought of it made me sick, but I agreed because at least if someone else was there then I knew the boys would be safe.

I felt that the whole system had let me down and that no one was there to protect my kids. I know that most fathers should have a right to see their children, but surely not if they have done something like this to them? I know it is not over yet. I feel upset and angry every time I think about the fact that he is going to get contact with the children, but I just have to take it one step at a time. I will only do what I think is best for the boys, so who knows what will have happened in a few months time.

Kate's story

I had been married for 24 years. The worst thing about the divorce was feeling as if I had failed somehow, because when you are married for that long you expect it to be for life. But no matter how much I tried, it was just me who was trying, he wasn't. It wasn't another woman or anything, we just grew apart. Men are very selfish. Mine wanted to keep the good lady at home with the family and expected to go out and about himself. Bill was music orientated, highbrow stuff, always off to choirs or band practice, but in the end enough was enough.

The final straw was that my daughter, who was 14 at the time, started rebelling against him. Bill had always pushed her in music, until she wasn't having a childhood but was always involved in piano and choirs and so on. When she started rebelling he just let me get on with it, as if to say 'it's all up to you now, Kate'. He made me feel I had to sort it out on my own. She was going out and not coming home when she said she would. I would wait at the bus stop crying and watching the buses going by. She would lie about where she was going. I know teenagers get rebellious but the atmosphere at home made it ten times worse. We were arguing over her all the time. As I say, it made me realise how selfish he was.

We also had a 2-year-old at the time. He'd wanted another baby when I was already 39, so we had one, but he didn't change one little bit. They say a leopard doesn't change its spots.

I kept making excuses for him, but then you wake up one day and think 'this isn't life'. He was very domineering, he wanted everything his way and it got to the stage where I couldn't put up with it any more. He wouldn't even take his own keys when he went out, knowing that that would force me to stay at home to let him in. He said he didn't like bulking his pockets but it was all about controlling me. He was out nearly every night of the week and I was left to get on with it. Some weekends he went off to some music conference or other, and he took holidays on his own, without me. I wouldn't be interested in going.

These were all things that I ended up putting on the divorce petition as examples of his unreasonable behaviour towards me.

Looking back now I was extremely lucky. I was at my lowest ebb, I looked in the phone directory and luckily I just picked a good solicitor. As soon as I'd been to see her, she took a weight off my shoulders. I was being treated as a person, and she immediately realised what I was going through, somebody understood at last. She boosted my confidence, and made me realise I was not a hundred per cent wrong.

He had managed to undermine me an awful lot. Everything I did was always wrong in his eyes. I am a Catholic as well, so you can imagine what it was like; I was the first person in the family to get a divorce. Luckily, though, I did get their support. It is amazing what people see but do not say. They started asking how I'd managed to stay married for so long, though they'd never said anything before for fear of interfering. The biggest step to take was definitely going to a solicitor. I found it very difficult because it was like finally admitting to everybody after 24 years that the marriage had failed.

My biggest worry was being on my own financially. I was only working from home doing market research part-time and my income was very limited. The finances were horrendous. I ended up going to court to sort it out. He did so many things I would never have imagined. Friends advised me to empty the joint bank account but I didn't; he got there first and emptied it. He took everything he could, even to the point of digging plants out of the garden! He wouldn't leave the home either. I had left the bedroom as soon as things weren't working and had been sleeping on a camp bed.

It was the courts that got him out of the house. He argued that he had nowhere to go, so to begin with I got an injunction where he stayed in the house but he was not allowed to be abusive. But then he slapped my daughter, and the courts said he had to leave the house. It was terrible. I'd even asked my sister to look after my daughter for a couple of months because the atmosphere was so bad, but once he was out my daughter came back home again.

In relation to the finances, the judge ordered Bill to pay me interim maintenance until things were sorted out. At the Final Hearing I decided I did not want anything for myself, I just wanted it for the children. We had shares, some money and property and the whole thing ended up being split about 50:50. Looking back, I feel it was fair: I could have got more but I wanted out as quickly as possible. He contested everything and I didn't want to haggle at the end of the day. Even now there are still problems and it's five years on!

With the contact issue, the two eldest would not see Bill, and they still don't to this day. That is their choice. The youngest sees him now, but that wasn't without problems because he would let her down on contact arrangements. She would be expecting daddy and daddy wouldn't come. Then he would fight through the courts and see a welfare officer, who recommended that we restart contact, but then he would just cancel again. We are still arguing over contact now! We went back to court just two months ago because this time he wants to take the youngest abroad, and I have said no, so we are arguing over that. He has also stopped my older daughter's maintenance because I now work full-time. She is at university and he owed me God knows how much in arrears but got it all revoked by the courts. Then in November he was back at court trying to stop my son's maintenance. I went to court on that one and this time they decided he has to pay. He did not get away with it this time.

The best advice I could give to anyone thinking about divorce is to get a good solicitor and to ask someone who has been divorced for a recommendation. You can look in the phone book, but it's better to ask someone who has had a divorce. I was very lucky. I had loads of confidence in my solicitor. She gave me my confidence back and made me realise I was not a failure. It was so good to come out and know you could get your self-worth back. It helped me straight away. I did have friends around but they were all biased. My solicitor told me things straight. I wanted to know where I stood and she told me. She said I would have trouble for years and I still do; only today I received some more court papers.

At the time I was worried sick about the finances and how I would cope with three children, but now I feel fantastic. My only regrets are not doing it sooner and being as gullible as I was with him, thinking he would not do half the things he did. He even cancelled all the insurances. I thought I was insured and I wasn't; you can't get much lower than that! But even so, the whole thing was well worth it in the long run. I am thankful to have got my life back and it was much better to get out for the children's sake. It is surprising what they pick up on, and you don't realise until afterwards. If I'd stayed I would have ended up losing my whole family, so in the end it was the best decision that I could ever have made.

Richard's story

I married Pamela 15 years ago and we divorced two and a half years ago. We had two children, one daughter of 19 and another of 14. I finally left home in July 1999.

What made me leave was suddenly finding out that my wife had been gambling all our money away, in slot machines. I thought things were fine financially, and that we had £7000 in our account, though to be honest I hadn't checked it because she was in charge of paying all the bills in our house.

It started when I first realised that certain bills were not getting paid. My daughter was at university and one day she rang and asked why her rent hadn't gone through. She said her mother had told her not to mention it to me, but she was worried. I couldn't understand it, I was earning well at the time and our joint income was about £52,000 a year.

I asked Pamela what was going on. She admitted there were one or two problems, which she promised to sort out, but I had no idea how serious things were. What I did know was that she had been going out regularly when I was working. I pushed her to tell me what had been going on and then she admitted it all. She told me that she had been spending all our money in slot machines! I told her she would have to get a grip of herself. I soon found out that she had a serious gambling addiction, in fact she had had it for years, and I had never even noticed! She had always looked after all our money matters.

I realised how bad the situation had got when I told her that I needed a new car and was planning to get one the following week. I still hadn't checked the account at this stage, but Pamela kept saying she didn't think it was a good idea. When I eventually went to the bank, there was nothing in it! We were in the red, and there was also a bank loan for £1000 that I knew nothing about and a washing machine debt I'd already given her the money for. To say I was upset was an understatement.

I got a month's statements there and then. She had been taking out a minimum of £250 a day. Every day I was working she had been on the slot machines. I ended up requesting seven years' worth of statements, and I went through them with a fine-toothed comb. I found out that in that time she had withdrawn a total of £120,000 in cash. I could not prove how much of that she had used for gambling, but I had been paying all the household bills by direct debit so the money hadn't gone on those things.

It all came out in the end. My eldest daughter had had an idea about it. Pamela was so desperate to get access to cash that at Christmas she always bought me things that were the wrong size. Then she would take them back to the shop and pocket the money. When I found out about everything I told her she had a problem, and said I would try to help her with it. She was not able to see that she had any sort of problem though. She still blames me for everything. She said I did not care about her, that I spent too much time on my hobbies and did not give her enough attention. There may be some truth in that, but we went on holiday all over the place. All my money went into the family and she had never complained about the way things were. I knew there were a few problems but I didn't think we were on the point of breaking up. I said I would help if she wanted me to; I said I would take control of the finances and I opened another account in my name which then paid all the bills. I told her all she had to buy with her own money was the food.

But from that moment on she got nasty because her money supply was cut off. She stopped buying food and started intercepting the mail and ripping up bills. The problem had not gone away, she carried on taking everything out of the hole in the wall, even the Child Benefit. The straw that finally broke the camel's back was that my daughter rang up and said there was no food in the house. By May I had decided to leave home. I told my daughters what I planned to do and the younger one said she wanted to come with me. I organised accommodation and then the two of us left home.

When I first went to see the solicitor I was highly emotional and blurted it all out. The solicitor brought me into sharp focus about how stupid I had been in the relationship. It made me face things a lot and made me a little bit harder about the way I felt. I was worried about the kids and how I would cope putting one of the children through university. I was petrified, wondering whether I could still live and provide for the kids. I was a gibbering wreck at work and it was my colleagues who helped me through it all. It wasn't the end of the marriage that concerned me by that stage, it was just how I was going to get through it all.

I filed for divorce based on her unreasonable behaviour. I felt I should also fight the financial situation but when I went to court the judge said that, regardless of Pamela's gambling problem, he was mindful that she was 52 years old with little working life left, and he was concerned that she had somewhere else to live. My barrister said we could either argue in court or we could give her the house and the endowments so she would have somewhere to live and settle things on that basis, so that is what we did. There was equity of £40,000 in the house and the endowments were worth £30,000. She got the lot. She also got the car, but I got to keep my pension, which was worth £180,000, and I was free from having to pay her maintenance. I had paid all the bills over the time before we got to court and paid off a lot of her debts, but I know from what I have heard that she still has the same problem with money.

Looking back I am now happy that I have got rid of the millstone round my neck, but I am disgusted that I got charged £5500 for the legal fees; I had been told it would be a lot less. I ended up one day with a bill not having been told it would be that much, so I feel really short-changed and disappointed about that. I knew there would be a cost, but the huge expense came as a result of my wife's thieving and embezzlement, and I ended up having to pay for it. In the long run though, my children have seen how much I have had to give up on their behalf so, although they have gone without, it has brought us really close together. That is the positive side of the whole thing.

Pamela sees our younger daughter, but a lot less frequently than the older one who is now a professional and visits her mother only occasionally. We never needed a Contact Order, it was just left up to the children to decide what they wanted. In any case, they were old enough to make up their own minds about it.

My advice to anyone would be to think seriously about the implications of going to the law to resolve anything. I was offered mediation and I turned it down because I thought it would take too long, but the law wasn't any quicker and at times the process was painfully slow. I thought it would all be much quicker than it was.

My advice would be to explore mediation before going to lawyers. I would say you are better off sorting things out between yourselves if you can face each other. I wish I had known how long it would take, the cost of it, and the implications of all the various legal steps. I was a police officer but I had no understanding of the legal process and was totally overwhelmed by it. The lawyers did not explain things enough to me. I feel I did 95 per cent of the work for the case myself. I provided all the information to the lawyers; all they did was put it all in a file and present it to the court. Most people have no concept of what a court is about, and you don't realise how awful you will feel on the day.

I have now bought my own house. My mortgage will last for years, but I am happy where I am. It has turned out really well and I couldn't ask for anything better. I won't settle with anyone else though. I work long hours, I have a daughter at home, and I spend a lot of time with her. I meet people and they are great but as soon as it gets a bit more complicated I can't face it and I back off, and I don't totally trust people any more. I feel happy to be on my own – I certainly wouldn't get married again. My overriding feeling is that if you are a white, middle-aged, middle-class male the whole world is against you. Sorry, but that is what I think. Life is less complicated on your own. Now if I want something I buy it and if I don't want to do something I don't do it. Now I have a bit more time for me.

Alicia's story

I was in a violent relationship for just over 18 months. When you're in that sort of situation it gets you down to such a level that you don't know how to get out of it. You blame yourself all the time and think it's all your fault, and that's exactly what I did.

Right from our wedding reception I'd realised that Robert had a problem with alcohol. He'd had a difficult upbringing, in which both parents had drunk huge amounts themselves. I know things may have been tough for him but I found him to be emotionally very weak. Whenever anything went even the slightest bit wrong he would get so drunk that he didn't know what he was doing.

When we got married, we already had one son who was about a year old and I was eight weeks pregnant with our second child. The violence started the day after the wedding. We'd already been together for about two years by the time we got married and we'd certainly had problems but there hadn't been any violence. I was only about 21, and looking back I probably shouldn't have got married in the first place, but I was too young to know any different.

The first time it happened Robert suddenly just looked at me and said: 'Don't look at me like that.' I didn't know what he meant at all, but he flew into such a rage and kicked me so hard that I ended up huddled in the corner of the room. I couldn't work out what I'd done, but I thought I must have done something otherwise this wouldn't have happened. Things just seemed to get worse from that day on. Once he had done it once it seemed that he would do it whenever he'd had a few to drink.

The pregnancy had given me a bad back and Robert used to kick me there because he knew it was where I was most vulnerable. I used to curl into a ball and he would just keep on kicking me until he'd had enough. It could be the slightest little thing that would trigger him off. It almost seems silly because Robert is only a small man, smaller than me even, but I never fought back; I just took it and waited for him to finish every time. When it was over I would just sit there, and he would storm off and leave the house and I would go to bed on my own.

It seemed to happen more and more often as time went on. I remember one particular day when I was seven months pregnant. I was sitting on the sofa knitting and I heard him come in from the pub. I froze because I was so frightened of what he would do. I was so scared I didn't know how to react or what to do and I didn't even dare look at him. For no reason at all he grabbed me by my hair, threw me to the floor and started kicking me again.

There was one period when things got better for a little while, when we went to Relate for counselling to try and sort things out between us. For those three months he didn't drink and the violence stopped. He started opening up and talking about things and for a while I thought maybe it would all get better. But then something happened at work to upset him and this triggered off his drinking again. That's when the violence started again. In the end I left Robert after we'd been married for about 18 months, when the baby was one.

I found it really hard to do anything about the situation, but I had one good female friend who I was able to talk to. She was the only person I told about it. I didn't know a single person who had been through anything like what I had suffered, and I found it almost impossible to tell anyone else because I was so embarrassed. I felt ashamed that this was happening to me and I didn't know how to stop it. Luckily he never hit the children but I felt as though that could have been the next step. I can't say that they didn't suffer though, because they witnessed what happened between us and there were occasions when he hit me even while I was holding the baby.

What saved me from all of this was the fact that I met someone else while I was still with Robert. He gave me the strength to leave, and to start believing that I didn't have to put up with this any longer.

The day it all finally finished I had just got ready to go out with the children and Robert grabbed me from behind and started slamming my head against the front door. I managed to get out of the house but I didn't dare go back for fear of what he would do next so I went round to my friend's house. She ended up going to my home and telling Robert to leave. The funny thing was that by the time she arrived he already has his bags packed and was ready to go. Perhaps he knew himself that this time he had gone one step too far. It didn't end there, though, because he got trashed and turned up at my door again at 3 o'clock the next morning. He was crying and said it was all his fault and he wanted me back. When I refused to talk to him he tried to get in and threw things at the window. I had to call the police, who came and removed him, but I heard later that he'd gone round to his dad's and trashed his house as well.

Looking back now I know that while the violence was going on I felt completely and utterly outside myself. I felt ashamed, weak and worthless. I was not a whole person and it sapped all of who I was. I just about managed to keep functioning, but there was no 'me', no personality, there was just a shell of a person left. It took a long, long time for all of that to come back even after the relationship was over.

I would love to give people advice about how to help someone in that situation, but the problem is you can't help someone who is not ready to help themselves. Until they can find a little bit of strength that will allow them to make that break and leave the situation, they will just keep going back. The only thing I can say is that you can come through it, and there are people out there to support you. It doesn't matter how bad the violence is, it always makes you feel the same way, it saps everything from you.

The only piece of advice I do have is don't be quiet about it. There are places like Women's Aid where they have people trained to deal with situations of domestic violence. They won't be surprised by anything you tell them. I wish I had known they were there when I was going through it, but at the time I didn't, and to be honest I don't know if I'd have said anything to them anyway. The other thing you can do is to tell your GP. You know that what you say will be in confidence and your GP shouldn't judge you. He or she should be able to give you advice as to where to turn next. If you're in the position where you feel that you just can't tell anyone because they will think it is all your fault, you need to be reassured that your life isn't right or normal, and that people will listen.

For me this all finished nine years ago. Now I feel as though it happened to a completely different person. I was nothing like I am now. Now I am much more confident, more determined and more assertive, I feel far healthier than I did then and I would never ever accept that type of behaviour from anyone again. The difference now is that I know that I don't have to take it. There is a choice, and you don't have to live with that kind of behaviour. In my case my GP recommended counselling, and I found a counsellor I could work with really well. It was hard and painful to go through counselling and talk about everything that had happened in the past but it was worth doing, because my life is much more sorted now.

Louise's story

The violence in our relationship went on for over 19 years.

It always started because Darren had to have his own way. He was incredibly domineering and pig-headed and would sulk if I didn't do what I was told. He would get moody and refuse to talk to me for days, which would put me totally on edge. He expected me to have his tea on the table at 5 o'clock every evening, even though I'd been working all day. I just wanted a quiet life so I tried to do whatever it took to please him. If I didn't I knew that he would just cut himself off again and not speak to me for days. When that happened it would always be me who tried to make up with him.

I first met him when I was 19. To begin with we each had our own flat, and we used to stay with each other several times a week. Things seemed to be going OK, but then after about six months we went out one evening and he bumped into an old girlfriend. I'd thought that we were staying together that night, but once Darren had met her he told me that I'd have to go back to my own flat because he was going to stay with her that night. I couldn't believe it. How could my boyfriend just announce that he was going home with another woman? I stood up to him and told him what I thought. His response was to slap me round the face. I said 'you'll never do that to me again', but he just laughed and did it a second time. That night my dad came and took me home. I was devastated.

Darren didn't ring me for ages and I thought things were all over between us, but then one day he rang again and apologised. He said he'd been drinking that night and was really sorry for what had happened. I went back to him, I suppose because I was still in love with him, and to begin with things weren't too bad between us.

Then after about a year it all started again. Before too long we had a baby and I realised he was a complete control freak. I wouldn't get in from work until 6.45 most nights, and when I got there he'd be moaning that there was nothing ready to eat. His mother would childmind for us and drop the baby off in the evenings. Darren would be fine in front of his mother but as soon as she'd gone, he'd have another go at me for not keeping the house tidy. He would never do any housework himself. If he saw dishes on the side, even if they were clean, he would smash them all on to the floor. He would tell me to get on my knees and clean it up and I would do it. If we were out together somewhere I would just know by a look that I was expected to behave in a certain way, and sometimes at home he would put a pillow over my face and say 'I could smother you if I wanted to'.

The problem was that I used to think it was me all the time. I must have been winding him up or doing something wrong for him to behave in this way, and despite it all I didn't want to split up from him. I suppose he must have had some sort of hold over me. I would look for his good points and say to myself at least he is strong and he will always look after me, even though he wasn't doing that at all. I just couldn't bear the thought of having to split up and being on my own again. In some ways I thought we were pretty well off. We had nice things in the house, and whereas my friends were all in debt we'd saved up for everything we owned and didn't owe anybody money, which I thought was a good thing too.

When it came to the finances generally Darren would make me pay for the food shopping out of my wages and all of his wages would go into the bank, in his sole name. I never had access to his account. I was never able to go to the shops and just buy something, I'd always have to ask for it first. Sometimes he would take the car keys from me and hide them so that I couldn't go out anywhere. I was allowed to see my mother at the weekend but not anyone else. I couldn't even ring her because Darren didn't want me to use the phone. He would say that I should wait until she rang me. I hardly had any friends of my own. I didn't know many people anyway and everyone who lived around us was a lot older. I definitely wasn't allowed to socialise with anyone else. I was incredibly isolated, but that is exactly what Darren wanted.

It's only now I'm older I can look back and see what he was doing. At the time though I didn't want to get divorced even though I wasn't happy because for some reason I felt like I had to stick it out. Darren had made me that dependent on him that I was frightened at the thought of being on my own.

During the 19 years we were together Darren would do something to me about once a week on average. Sometimes it was just an elbow in the back or a push, but every six months or so there would be a really serious attack. On one occasion he pulled me down the stairs by my hair, jumped on my hand and broke my fingers. That time it was because I'd said I was too tired to go out that night. He started sulking about it so I changed my mind and agreed to go out, but then he just said 'Don't bother, I'm going out without you'. He left me at the bottom of the stairs, put his jacket on, went out and didn't come back for two days. When he did he was full of remorse and said it would never happen again, but of course it did.

Sometimes he would take my favourite items of clothing, anything that he thought made me look attractive, and cut them up. He must have done that in total twenty or thirty times. That was just another way of controlling me. The worst thing, though, were the mind games. When he wasn't being violent he would say that I was big, fat and lazy, that I had a fat arse because I sat on it all day long. He would say I had got pregnant on purpose to trap him and that I was a slag. He would also spit in my face. That was his favourite. That was the most humiliating thing he could have done but I didn't know what I could do about it. He made me absolutely paranoid about myself. He told me all the time that I looked disgusting, so that is how I ended up feeling.

Looking back I don't think he ever loved me, though other people say maybe he did and just didn't know how to show it. I think we were just stuck together by our two children. I can see why people will think that I should have left, but I had a nice house and a nice life in other ways. He used to say to me that if I left I would go with nothing, and I believed him. I didn't know what my rights were.

My worst regret is that my son was witness to some of the violence and he will never forget it. On one occasion Darren pulled me down the stairs and kicked me in the stomach and Josh saw everything. I was shouting at him to go upstairs and stay in his bedroom and he was screaming with fright. I know that seeing things like that must have been terrible for him.

All in all I ended up in hospital about five times. He broke my arm once by pulling me out of the house. That time I had been trying to stop him shutting the door on me and as he slammed the door on to me I fell over and cracked it on the footpath. Most times when I went to the hospital I just lied and made up a story about what had happened. I would say I had fallen over or something. I was too embarrassed to tell the truth because I didn't want people to know what was going on. I thought because I'd argued back I must have brought it all on myself. I always avoided getting medical help unless it was urgent that I got treatment. One time I needed stitches in my eye and another time I had to go after he perforated my eardrum by punching me in the head.

I hardly confided in anyone about what things were really like at home. I did tell my mother once after he'd thrown me out of the house. He had driven home after drinking a lot, and arrived back completely wasted. I had called him an idiot for being a drunk driver. His response was to throw me out into the cold in my pyjamas. Then he just went to bed and ignored me. I was standing in the street freezing cold and shouting at him to let me back in, but he just ignored me. A neighbour telephoned my parents and my mum picked me up and tried to persuade me not to go back. That night I told her everything. She was furious about all the things he had done to me, and the next day she gave him hell. Darren didn't speak to her for ten years after that.

I know about helplines and things now, but a few years ago I wasn't really aware of what was available. The police offered to help me find a place in a refuge a few times but I couldn't do it. I felt guilty because the kids would have lost their home. I knew they shouldn't be living with this sort of violence but I justified my decision by saying that most of the violence happened when they were in bed. I thought if I left him I would have nothing, no money, no house and no car. I couldn't bear the thought of a refuge, but I wish I had done it now. At the time I felt that my situation couldn't be as bad as it was for other people, the people who really needed refuges. I thought that if I could just do things right I would be able to keep Darren happy and things would be OK.

As I got older I started thinking that it wasn't right to live like this. I heard about all the nice things my friends' husbands would do for them and wondered why it was never like that for me. He didn't ever bother much at Christmas. I would always get him a Valentine's card but he never got me one. He used to ask what the point was.

What made me leave in the end was meeting someone else. When I first met Sam at work we just chatted and I thought he was so nice; not just to me but to other people. I couldn't believe how nice he was. We went out one Christmas and I spent the whole evening wondering how a man could be as nice as that. It took ages before we started seeing each other. He had met Darren and thought he was an arrogant pig and asked me why I was with him. I wasn't really sure myself.

I spent 19 years trying to do everything I possibly could to make Darren happy. I made all his meals, cleaned the house, went to work and then laboured for him in the evenings on the houses we had bought to do up to get money in for the family, but there was no affection, loving or kindness back from him. When we eventually got divorced he even tried to belittle me in all the court papers by saying that I had never done anything in the house, or made any effort for the family when nothing could have been further from the truth.

The last Christmas we were together he didn't buy me a present, or anything for my birthday which was a couple of weeks later. He just went out with his friends and I was left on my own. Everyone at work was asking what I'd got for my birthday and I had to say nothing. Sam couldn't believe it, and on the following Monday when I went to work he had bought me a gold necklace because he said no one should go without any presents on their birthday.

That was it. That was when I realised there was something better out there. I started saying to Darren that things weren't right but he would just laugh and say 'You won't get any money from me'. I tried to be amicable about things but he took the car keys and the house keys so I couldn't even go out unless he was there.

In the end I went to see a solicitor just by picking one from the Yellow Pages. When I told my solicitor about things at home she said that nobody should have to live like that. She wrote Darren a letter but when he received it he went ballistic, and that's when the worst incident of violence happened. It was my daughter who eventually said if you don't go now I'm going on my own. She was only 13 and she had already packed all her bags. Both kids were completely fed up with the situation and just wanted to be out of it. That made me think seriously that we would all be better off out of it, even if it meant ending up with nothing financially.

To begin with I moved into my mother's house. We took clothes and nothing else. We stayed with her for two months, and then we stayed at a friend's house for a few weeks. During that time my solicitor applied for an Occupation Order. It seemed to take ages for it to come through. I had to go to court to get it. Darren was there with his father and he was really arrogant all the way through. I also found out that he had been taping all my phone calls over the past three months. He had got a private investigator to tap the phone, so he had known all my plans and tried to spoil them. I had been confiding in my best friend, all of which he heard, so he would tell me that she was spreading gossip about me to everyone in the village. She hadn't at all, it was just because he had heard our calls and wanted me to distrust her and ruin our friendship.

After the Occupation Order was made he would come round every night and scream at me on the street. All the neighbours knew our business, so I had to go back to court and get an injunction. When he broke it he was given a suspended sentence for six months. He used to stay outside the house and say 'You wait until the six months is over, I'm going to come and get you'. He has broken the injunction again since, but at the moment I just can't bear the thought of going back to court again. If he does anything again I suppose I will have to go back until he leaves me alone.

The mistake Darren made was that he thought if I left that he would end up with everything. He never believed I would be brave enough to go to a solicitor and fight for my rights through the courts.

Now that it's all over I feel relieved. The financial side of things has been sorted out, I ended up with over 60 per cent of everything and I am going to buy my own house and start again. Even now, though, I have to be honest and say that in a way I am sad I had to get divorced. I still feel free though. The funny thing is that what hurt Darren more than anything was the fact that I got money out of the marriage. I feel that when I move and get my own place he won't have a hold on me any more and I am really looking forward to starting again. My boyfriend has suggested that we buy a house together but I'm not sure whether I am ready for that. I am still really insecure about men, even though I know that Sam is not Darren. I just don't want anything like that again. I still feel a little bit sorry for Darren. He's got no one now and has lost most of his friends.

It's hard to give advice to anyone. I can only say there is never any real need to stay. You never need to stick it out, it will always be better to go, but you have to do it for your own peace of mind. It is so nice to go to bed at night and know I will not end up with a pillow on my head or an elbow in my back or be turfed out in the middle of the night. That is lovely.

I would just say to anyone in that situation to talk to someone about it. There are so many groups out there that can help. I couldn't have done it at the time, but now I have more information, I wish that I had known who to call to get some reassurance and advice as to what to do next. I spent years absolutely convinced that I would get nothing financially if I left him because that is what Darren had told me, and that was completely wrong. I would definitely say to anyone reading this to ring someone and talk to them. I kept it all to myself for years and I regret that now. Doing what I did was hard, but it wasn't as bad as I thought it was going to be, and I am proud now that I did it all. I wanted to be free and now I am, and that is a good feeling.

Max's story

My position is that I already have the decree nisi but I am still waiting for the absolute to arrive.

The whole process started in March of last year when I told June that the marriage was over. The formal proceedings started in May. The divorce took seven months from start to finish so it wasn't too long. I am now 58, June is 56 and we had been married for 33 years. We have two adult daughters who at the time were 30 and 24.

What made me end the marriage, or the final straw if you like, was that we had lived and worked overseas for 30 years, moving around all the time. When we finally came back to England, we did what we had always planned to do, which was to buy an old property, do it up and run it as a guest house. We did that for about two and a half years and then she suddenly said she was fed up with it, she said she wanted to sell it and do something completely different, though she couldn't tell me what. We seemed to have spent years always thinking that things would be better somewhere else. I was happy doing it but I realised that this problem would never go away, to my wife the grass was always greener. She had also suffered from depression for the past 20 years. She had been to a psychiatrist for therapy but that had not helped the depression.

I had tried very hard to make things better but I failed. For a long time I felt that things were my fault but I don't any more. When I said that I had had enough and we finally parted, we went to Relate for eight to ten sessions, and during those sessions a lot of things about the past became clearer. Going to Relate was never about patching things up between us, it was because my elder daughter had said that she wanted me to try to get my wife on to a more even keel as the two of them had not got on well for ages. She thought that it might help June come to terms with the fact that I was pulling out.

I did not find going to a solicitor difficult. I found it easy to do. My wife had already been to her solicitor and filed for divorce on the grounds of my adultery so I was responding to that. I did not defend the divorce because I just wanted it over. We had agreed between us that the marriage was over. Technically the process for me was easy but emotionally I found it difficult particularly because of the reaction of my elder daughter, who was quite hostile to the divorce. She understood why I wanted to leave but was incensed that there was another party involved. My younger daughter was very supportive.

When it came to the finances June and I managed eventually to agree matters without going to court but there was a heavy involvement of lawyers. I did not want to waste money on legal fees for something that could have been agreed early on with much lower costs, but she chose an expensive lawyer who advised her to do various things that were not only counter-productive, but she knew I would never agree to. Luckily my lawyer was reasonable and said there was no point in her getting over-involved if we could sort it out between ourselves.

In the end my legal fees were about £1000 for the whole thing whereas hers were nearer £4000. Her solicitor advised her to get specialist advice from an expert. She had to pay for all of that and the advice was to make an offer that I would never have agreed to. I had told her my proposal so she knew what my position was but she insisted on getting legal advice. I think she felt more vulnerable than I did, even though she had taken advice on the matter from other people. I fear her solicitor led her by the nose. He wrote letters at the drop of a hat and made ridiculous offers, every one of which she had to pay for. They tried to get me to pay her fees but I refused and they gave up in the end. The result was a clean break settlement. She will get 50 per cent of my pension and 53 per cent of the rest.

Looking back on the divorce I didn't think much about the whole thing. I just got on with it and thought I would deal with the problems afterwards. The biggest issue for me was the timing of it; how to deal with my wife and how she would react. My lawyer was absolutely superb, very down to earth, full of common sense and un-grasping. She was super and told me everything I needed to know about the process. I can't fault her.

My advice is that if you want to get divorced then do it now rather than in 20 years' time. Personally I should have done it much sooner but I didn't because of the children. Because I worked abroad I would never have ended up getting custody and was not prepared to leave them with an unstable mother. I am just glad now that the whole thing is over and dealt with.

Jackie's story (continued from page 18)

To give him his due, he'd worked hard all his life. I didn't want to take him to the cleaners, but that didn't mean I should be left homeless. All I wanted at the end of the day was to get the house. He told me over and over again that I would get nothing from the marriage, and to begin with I believed him. I was a meek little housewife then: he said jump and I jumped; I did what I was told.

I wish it could have been sorted out amicably but that wasn't possible in our case. I tried to be fair when we divorced, but because he wouldn't listen and spent so long fighting he ended up wasting thousands on his legal bills. Luckily my solicitor thought I had a good chance of winning and convinced me that it was worth fighting for. In the end the whole thing went to court and the judge decided that I would get the house, and that Geoff had to pay off the outstanding mortgage. He got the rest.

The fight to get what I was entitled to and to keep the house for the boys and me was hard but it was definitely worth the effort. I'm 55 now and I remarried 10 years ago. Things are fine now, though I do still wonder what it would have been like to have had a career. In some ways I feel that he took that from me. Sometimes people forget that women often give up a lot to make the marriage work.

My advice to anyone thinking about divorce is to be strong and know what you want. Even if you don't feel up to fighting for your entitlement it is worth doing, as if you give up you will regret it in the long run.

Janine's story

I got divorced five years ago now, after 18 years of marriage, and we had three children, a boy of 15 and daughters of 12 and 9.

By the time we separated the relationship between James and me had broken down completely, though things had been difficult for more than 10 years. Basically we just didn't talk any more, and we had less and less in common as time went on. I decided to go to university as a mature student to further myself and that is when it all went wrong.

He did everything he could to try and stop me getting on with what I wanted to do. First he moved out and left me with the children, but then he started pestering me by coming over to the house literally every morning and every afternoon, always on some sort of pretext. He wouldn't leave me alone. He just couldn't cope with us being separated. Then he started making suicide threats. It was awful. He used all sorts of emotional blackmail. I ended up moving out of the house with the children and we moved into rented accommodation, which cost a fortune. I only had a student grant to live on so things were very hard and I got into a lot of debt as a result.

Once we had been apart for two years I decided to file for divorce on the basis of two years' separation. After a few months I started seeing someone else, and though I was happy I felt incredibly guilty that my ex was still on his own. Because of that I took nothing from the home and had to start again from scratch. My ex then gave up his job and refused to work. He almost had a nervous breakdown, and I ended up on benefits. I found it heartbreaking to see someone that I had cared about in such a state, and it would have been easy to go back, but I just couldn't. I was determined not to.

I have to say, though, that I found the studying extremely hard both emotionally and financially. I also found that first trip to a solicitor very difficult. Once I'd told him about my situation the solicitor advised me that I could almost certainly ask for the house to be sold, and that I would probably get two-thirds of the proceeds as it was me who had care of the children. The problem was that I felt so guilty already that I knew I wouldn't be able to live with myself if I did that, so I decided to let him keep the house and I took nothing for myself. I genuinely thought that if I had forced a sale of the house that he might have ended up taking his own life.

Looking back now, though, I feel as if he has everything and he just played with my emotions to get what he wanted. I don't regret the divorce but I do regret the decisions I made over the house and the finances. I tried to be as amicable as possible throughout the whole thing, but the latest thing I have heard is that he doesn't even intend to leave the house to our children when he dies, but to one of his new partner's children instead. That I find really hurtful and to be honest it has made me furious. We put a lot of work into that house, and for all the right reasons – for the children. Now it seems as though they will get nothing.

I am not a materialistic person, but there were certain things I would like to have had, like some of our thousands of photos. There was one specific photo I asked him for, a picture of me on my wedding day with my father who has passed away now. He wouldn't even let me have that, and I still feel as though he just can't let things go.

My advice to anyone would be to try as hard as you can to put your emotions to one side when you are negotiating the finances and think very carefully about the long term. I allowed myself to be emotionally blackmailed and now I deeply regret that. The other thing I have learned is that it wasn't right to do as so many people do and stay 'for the sake of the children'. I realise now that it was the younger ones who coped far better with the divorce than the older one did. It was totally the wrong reason to stay together for so long, and there is a part of me that wishes I had been able to separate from him earlier. In relation to contact with the children, though, I do think it is important that a father should be allowed to see his children, whatever he has done. I know many people who won't allow their ex-husbands any contact and they do it just out of spite, which I think is totally wrong.

David's story

Even now when I look back I'm still not really sure why our marriage broke down. I'd been married to Sue for 18 years when it went wrong. We started having arguments all the time, and Sue would just go out every evening without telling me where she was going. Sometimes she stayed out all night and I had no idea where she was. She would also accuse me of all sorts bad behaviour. She thought I was seeing other women all the time when that simply wasn't true. I once went on a business trip to Jordan and she even accused me of marrying someone else while I was there! It was all complete rubbish but her suspicions made my life a living hell. We both come from large families and she spread all sorts of rumours about me among her family members. Needless to say, I got to hear about most of them. It got so bad that I moved away for a bit to see if things would calm down. What actually happened though was that every time I went round to the house to see her she would call the police to say I had been threatening her. She called them so many times that in the end they got fed up with it. They knew that she was just wasting police time. Then one day she called me on my mobile and said she had a surprise for me. I thought maybe she wanted to patch things up again, so I got to the house as soon as I could. When I arrived I discovered that she had taken out every single thing that we owned. Every item of furniture, all my personal possessions, and even the carpets. I have never got any of my things back even to this day.

I ended up moving in with my brother, but she knew where I was and every time she saw my car outside his house she would cause trouble. She would report me to the police for something I hadn't done, and on one occasion she even tried to drive into my car with hers. Her actions became so irrational that by the time I approached my solicitor it came as a relief. I didn't find it a difficult step at all. I filed for divorce on the grounds of her unreasonable behaviour. Her response at first was to waste as much time as she could by not responding to the divorce papers. I had to get them served on her by a bailiff. Then when she eventually did respond she refused to admit anything and denied all the allegations. She filed her own divorce petition and we ended up in court over it. In the end we divorced each other on cross petitions without any admissions being made by either of us.

At the moment I am still waiting for the decree nisi to come through, and it should arrive any day. The biggest headache is going to be sorting out all the finances. There is no way she will agree to any sort of reasonable settlement so I am sure that we will end up in court over it all. I come from a family of business people who between them own several different companies. Her tactic will be to accuse me of having a stake in lots of business ventures even though she knows that they are nothing to do with me. I don't really know what she wants from me financially so I suppose I will just have to wait and see.

I have to admit that I do feel bitter about everything that has happened; I have been to hell and back this past year, but now I have got to the stage where I just want this all to be over. I want to be able to get on with my life again, but I know that I won't even be able to start doing that until this whole process is behind me. That day cannot come soon enough.

Joanne's story

It was a nightmare. I had been married to Peter for 18 years; I was 42, and we had three children aged 16, 13 and 9. It is still all very raw as the divorce only went through a few weeks ago.

It all started because Peter wanted to have more freedom in his life, he wanted to come and go as he pleased. He even wanted a self-contained area within the house because he could not cope with our teenage girls going through puberty. He said he wanted this for ten years or thereabouts, until the girls had left home. I said this was ridiculous and unreasonable. He already had loads of freedom; he was self-employed and played golf, cricket and tennis. He even had a collection of jukeboxes – that was his hobby. But despite all of that he insisted on having this self-contained area. I told him this was unacceptable but not quite that calmly. In the end he thought that if he held out I would just go along with it, but I decided I didn't want at fiftysomething to realise I didn't want to be with the person I was married to.

The final straw was that he started to come in at four in the morning. He had no respect really; I was made to feel either stupid or insignificant, and I thought I am not prepared to go on living like this. I filed the divorce petition on 14 February! By October we had the decree absolute.

We were living in the same house during all of this and we are still in the same house now, even though we are already divorced. I have had to go to court on the finances, and to get an order that the house be sold because he would not agree to it otherwise. Things dragged on because he refused all the way through to get a solicitor, and even the judge was annoyed because he had not complied with any of the court orders.

In the end the judge ordered that I should get a 60:40 split on the first £420,000 of the proceeds of the house when it is sold, and 50:50 thereafter. We have to sell because neither of us has enough to buy the other out. Peter kept the jukeboxes, I got one endowment policy and he got the other. I got the bigger share because I have the children, and it is a clean break settlement so he doesn't have to pay me maintenance. He argued in court that the settlement should be 50:50 even though the children were staying with me. I have worked all through the marriage but I felt that that went against me in the end really. I was devastated. I had worked much harder than him during our marriage, but he started off by asking the court to make me pay maintenance to him! I am only a nurse, I don't earn that much. I am not a lawyer! But at least he dropped that in the end.

In relation to contact he does not seem to be interested. He says that I have no parenting skills but then he just ignores the kids himself, and my eldest daughter has ended up being poorly through all of this. I tried for an Occupation Order twice, which would have got him out of the house, but did not get one. Instead the judge divided the house between us so that he had his areas and I had mine. I was devastated about that. It was not fair because my eldest is on antidepressants and sleeping tablets and has self-harmed, and the youngest was having trouble going to school. He should have been made to leave, but it seemed that every legal step I was advised to take got me nowhere. It feels like a long, long time when you are living in that sort of environment.

When you read what people do for revenge you can understand it, but I did none of that, I played it by the book. He, on the other hand, took handles off doors so I couldn't get through them, built a wall down the middle of the conservatory, put builders' rubbish in the house, and said he would never leave the house. He threatened me, ignored the kids and, even though he was ordered by the court to get the house ready for sale, he ignored that as well. The house is up for sale now but I have taken out an astronomical bridging loan of £270,000 in order to get my kids away from here. I have bought somewhere without him knowing and I am moving there this week. I felt forced into doing that to get away from this atmosphere.

Somehow if he had been violent it would have been easier, I could have dealt with that. But now I feel that my 16-year-old is still crumbling, she has been off school for eight weeks and I am forced to take out this loan because he refuses to leave.

The advice I would give to anyone in this situation is don't wait 20 years before doing it, and don't expect to get rewards if you play it by the book. I would also say that in the end your peace of mind and the ability to shut your own front door is worth more than money. I do feel, however, that this whole process has been unjust. I feel like Peter was only ever interested in his own well-being, and didn't care what happened to me or the kids – that was a horrible lesson to learn. I cannot believe that the man I had been with for 20 years is the creature I have lived with for the past year.

The most shocking thing is how stupid I feel I have been. I come from the first generation of women who could have both family and career, but I feel we have shot ourselves in the foot.

For me it has meant that I have ended up even more controlled than my mother's generation was. Working and being independent, but still being responsible for the bulk of the childcare, is not independence at all. We are too busy doing both and juggling it all up in the air to realise what is happening. All the arguments about it being sensible for the bills to come out of my account meant that in the end I was far less liberated than someone who was actually given housekeeping, and the more you cope with the more you are expected to cope with. You have three kids and then you have another one in your husband.

In my job I run a team of nurses and have to sort out their problems daily but I couldn't see what was right in front of me. If Peter had been an employee I would have sacked him years ago! Everyone then says I could have told you all this years ago, but the hardest thing is accepting that you only have two choices: one is put up with it and the other one is don't, and neither is an easy choice. When you come to get divorced, if your husband has slept with someone else then somehow that is OK. People can understand that, but if it is a loose 'I want to find myself' then the decision you take will affect everyone else, and it is very, very hard.

The decision to get divorced was the hardest thing I have ever done. At the end of the day is it better to put up with it or realise this is not a healthy thing and get out of it? Having said that, I do not regret the decision I made. I wish I had done it before, but I did not believe myself to be important enough. What right did I have to alter the lives of four other people in addition to my own? But tomorrow's women will be more self-aware and informed of their own worth.

Looking back now I wish I had known more about the emotional trauma I was going to feel. It is like a bereavement process that you have to go through. Luckily I got on with my solicitor. When I was very, very bad, and not coping with the things that Peter was doing and saying, it was my solicitor who managed to put it in perspective for me. She even told me that when we went to court I should get a waterproof mascara that didn't run!

People can be flippant about how easy a divorce is, but they don't realise how difficult it can be. I would far rather have had some kind of civilised relationship with my ex, but that will never happen now because the whole thing has been so bitter.

I wish I had understood the legal process better than I did. It is so easy for lawyers to drop into legalese. The terminology and jargon is complicated. I wish I had known that I was allowed to talk; sometimes they all just talk over you and you can easily feel intimidated by lawyers about your own case! They start talking about things and there is a huge time pressure to make important decisions.

Contact is still an issue. What will happen if he wants contact? Does there have to be a Residence Order?

My advice would be stay on top of your costs, be aware of what they are and keep asking, don't get taken by surprise. It could cripple you if you don't. I wish I'd known about the costs because this whole thing ended up costing me about ten grand because everything was contested. That is horrific. It cost me more because he would not get himself a lawyer and he was contesting everything. He even got Legal Aid and I feel that is disgusting because he earns more than he said he did. I have had to pay and that is not fair.

If you are advised to take some form of legal action, make sure you know how much it will cost and whether it is likely to be worth doing. The law doesn't always help. I didn't want any of this, but in order to safeguard my children I had to fight. Looking back now, I think I wouldn't have been quite so reasonable. What I should have done was kick him out and change the locks and then let him fight me to get back in, but I still wanted the kids to have a relationship so I built his bridges for him and in return he just slagged me off to anyone who would listen. It was never my intention to fleece him, I wanted to be fair, but I had to fight for what I thought was fair.

This whole thing has taught me that there are fundamental differences between men and women. I would have appreciated knowing a little more of what to expect before it happened. My priorities now are to get my house, shut the front door and sort the kids out, and to repair the damage that has been done to all of them – and they are damaged. Now I am just grateful that it is all over. But I don't think any of it has been fair. It is very, very unfair, but to hang on to it would be to fester away, so I have to just let go, because ultimately it is worth it. If I had come away with nothing I would still rise again like phoenix from the ashes, but I can see why people get very bitter.

A Final Word

You will have seen that the stories in this chapter are all very different and that the people who told them all coped with the divorce process in their individual ways. We hope though that one common theme has come through in them all – while sorting out a divorce can be a difficult and painful experience, it can be made a lot easier by talking to someone and getting proper advice about what legal steps are open to you. We hope that this book will have provided the answers to at least some of the questions that you may have had about divorce, and we wish you every success with whatever personal decisions may lie ahead.

GLOSSARY

Absent parent The parent who is not living with the children of the marriage.

Acknowledgement of Service The form that the Respondent will have to fill in when he receives the divorce petition to prove that he has received it.

Adultery This is when your spouse has full sexual intercourse with another person during the time that you are still married.

Ancillary relief The term used to describe the whole process involved in sorting out the finances following a divorce.

Attachment of Earnings Order An order made when an order for maintenance (for either a spouse or the children) is not adhered to. This order deducts maintenance payments directly from a person's salary to ensure the person receiving maintenance is paid.

Barrister A type of lawyer who might give written advice on your case or represent you if you need to go to court.

Calderbank Offer A written offer made by your solicitor to your ex's solicitor prior to the Final Hearing. If you end up 'beating' this offer at court, you may end up winning back some of your legal costs.

Child Support Agency This is the agency that calculates how much maintenance the absent parent should pay in order to support his (or her) children.

Clean break Either an agreement or a court order on the finances that cuts any further financial ties or responsibilities between the parties.

Co-respondent The person that your spouse has committed adultery with (if adultery is your ground for divorce and you choose to name him or her on the divorce petition).

Con A shortened form of the word 'conference', which simply means a meeting between a client and a barrister.

Consent Order An agreement reached when two parties (usually ex husband and wife) manage to reach a settlement without the need for a contested court hearing. This is often done through negotiation between solicitors.

Contact This is what used to be known as 'access', in other words the way in which the absent parent will see or keep in touch with the children. Contact can be either face to face (direct contact) or by way of letters and cards (indirect contact).

Counsel Another term for a barrister.

Decree absolute The final stage of the divorce process. You are not divorced until the decree absolute has been granted.

Decree nisi The first court order you need to allow you to get a divorce. The decree nisi is granted when the judge is satisfied that the grounds for a divorce have been proved.

Desertion One of the grounds for divorce, where your spouse has left you with no good reason, without your consent and with the intention that the marriage is at an end. (See Chapter 4, page 49.)

Divorce petition The first document that is filed with the court to get a divorce underway. This details the reasons why you feel that the marriage is at an end.

Domiciled You are domiciled in the country where your permanent home is.

Enforcement proceedings Enforcement proceedings will be brought when there is already a court order in force and it is being disobeyed. A court will have various ways in which to ensure that the order is carried out in the way that it should be.

Equity This is the amount of money your house is worth minus any amounts still owing on it. To find the value of the equity, you need the full value of the house (you may need a valuation for this), then you take away the whole of the outstanding mortgage. The sum you are left with is the equity.

Family court adviser An independent person who helps the court reach a decision on matters to do with the children, such as where they should live and how much contact they should have with the absent parent.

Financial Dispute Resolution The second type of financial hearing when matters are being resolved at court. (See Chapter 7, pages 90–94.)

Former matrimonial home The term used to describe the house that a husband and wife last lived in as a couple.

Habitually resident You are habitually resident for the purposes of divorce in England and Wales if you have lived here for a year on the date the divorce petition is filed.

Injunction See Non-molestation Order.

Interim Order A court order that is intended to last for a limited period only until a final decision can be made. Examples of cases when Interim Orders can be made are maintenance, residence, contact or occupation cases.

Legal Aid Franchise This means that a firm of solicitors is able to represent clients under the Legal Aid scheme.

Legal Services Commission The new term for the Legal Aid Board.

Maintenance Money paid by one former spouse to another in regular intervals to support the ex-spouse and/or the children. It is also known as periodical payments.

Maintenance Pending Suit A temporary maintenance order where you are requesting your spouse to pay you maintenance until the final financial order is made by the court.

Matrimonial asset Anything (whether property, money, shares or policies) that was owned by either or both of you during the course of the marriage.

Mediation A process designed to help separating or divorcing couples discuss and make final decisions on their future arrangements, for example on finances and the children. It is described fully in Chapter 6.

Non-molestation Order A court order requiring someone to fulfil certain obligations, such as staying away from you, or not threatening or harassing you in any way. Also called an injunction.

Occupation Order A court order that decides who should live in the home.

Parental responsibility The term used to describe all the rights and responsibilities that a parent has towards the children. The mother has it automatically, and a father can get it by agreement, marrying the child's mother or through a court order.

Periodical payments See Maintenance.

Petitioner The person, either husband or wife, who first starts off the divorce proceedings and files the divorce petition at court.

Prohibited Steps Order An order made in relation to children preventing a person from doing something he would otherwise be able to do as someone with parental responsibility for the child.

Property Adjustment Order An order made by the court that allocates property between the parties in the case. For example, an order saying that the marital home should become the sole property of the wife would fall into this category.

Residence Order This used to be called 'custody', and is a court order that decides where the children should live.

Respondent The person, either husband or wife, to whom the divorce petition is sent when the Petitioner starts proceedings.

Separation For the purposes of divorce, separation is when you are no longer living with your spouse as husband and wife. This can either be in separate households or under the same roof. (See Chapter 4.)

Solicitor The lawyer who you will first approach as soon as you know you need legal advice. Your solicitor will also negotiate, write letters and prepare court documents on your behalf, as well as instructing a barrister if you need one.

Specific Issue Order An order that decides a 'specific issue' concerning a child in connection with how parental responsibility should be exercised, e.g. where a child should go to school.

Spouse Your husband or wife.

Statement of Arrangements The form that must be filed with the divorce petition if there are any children of the marriage and deals with any future arrangements concerning the children.

Undertaking A promise to the court to do (or not do) certain things which is one step short of a court order.

Unreasonable behaviour The term often used to describe one of the grounds for divorce. It refers to a situation where your spouse has behaved in such a way that you can no longer be expected to live with him. (See Chapter 4.)

Welfare checklist This is a list of the things that a court will have to take into account before making a Residence or Contact Order concerning a child. (See Chapter 8, pages 112–113.)

USEFUL ADDRESSES

Child Benefit Centre
Telephone: 08701 555540

Child Support Agency
Contact the enquiry line for details of regional offices.
National enquiry line: 08457 133 133
Web site: www.csa.gov.uk

Children's Legal Centre
University of Essex
Wivenhoe Park
Colchester
Essex C04 3SQ
Telephone: 01206 873820
Web site: www.childrenslegalcentre.com

Community Legal Service Leaflet Line
To obtain a leaflet on family law issues for divorcing couples
Telephone: 0845 3000343
Web site: www.justask.org.uk
To obtain the booklet *My Family's Splitting Up* or a leaflet entitled
Parenting Plan write to
FREEPOST
PO Box 2001
Burgess Hill
West Sussex RH15 8BR
Web site: www.lcd.gov.uk

Families Need Fathers
134 Curtain Road
London EC2A 3AR
Telephone: 020 7613 5060
Web site: www.fnf.org.uk

Family Mediators Association
Telephone: 020 7881 9400
Web site: www.familymediators.co.uk

Gingerbread
The organisation for one-parent families.
7 Sovereign Close
Sovereign Court
London E1W 3HW
Telephone: 020 7488 9300
Advice line: 0800 018 4318
Web site: www.gingerbread.org.uk

The Law Society of England and Wales
113 Chancery Lane
London WC2A 1PL
Telephone: 020 7242 1222
Web site: www.lawsoc.org.uk

Legal Services Commission
85 Gray's Inn Road
London WC1X8TX
Telephone: 020 7759 1131
Helpline: 0845 608 1122
Web site: www.legalservices.gov.uk

London Marriage Guidance
76a New Cavendish Street
London W16 9TE
Telephone: 020 7580 1087
Web site: www.londonmarriageguidance.org.uk

NSPCC
Weston House
42 Curtain Road
London EC2A 3NH
Telephone: 020 7825 2500
Helpline: 0800 800 5000
Web site: www.nspcc.org.uk

National Association of Child Contact Centres
Minerva House
Spaniel Row
Nottingham NG1 6EP
Telephone: 0870 770 3269
Web site: www.naccc.org.uk

National Council for One Parent Families
255 Kentish Town Road
London NW5 2LX
Head Office telephone: 020 7428 5400
Helpline: 0800 018 5026
Web site: www.oneparentfamilies.org.uk

National Family Mediation
9 Tavistock Place
London WC1H 9SN
Information line: 020 7485 8809
Administration: 020 7485 9066
E-mail: general@nfm.org.uk
Web site: www.nfm.u-net.com

National Family and Parenting Institute
430 Highgate Studios
53–79 Highgate Road
London NW5 1TL
Telephone: 020 7424 3460
Web site: www.nfpi.org.uk

One Parent Families
Helpline: 0800 018 5026

PDT Family Mediators
Telephone: 0800 028 4638

Parentline Plus
520 Highgate Studios
53–79 Highgate Road
London NW5 1TL
Head Office telephone: 020 7284 5500

Helpline: 0808 800 2222
Web site: www.parentlineplus.org.uk

The Principal Registry of the Family Division
Family Proceedings Department
First Avenue House
42–49 High Holborn
London WC1V 6NP
Telephone: 020 7947 6000
Web site: www.courtservice.gov.uk/fandl/prob_guidance.htm

Refuge 24-hour Domestic Violence Helpline
Helpline: 08705 995443

Relate
Herbert Gray College
Little Church Street
Rugby CV21 3AP
Telephone: 01788 573241
Web site: www.relate.org.uk

Reunite
Advice line: 0116 255 6243
Web site: www.reunite.com

Samaritans
PO Box 9090
Stirling FK8 2SA
Helpline (24 hours): 08457 909090
Web site: www.samaritans.org

Solicitors Family Law Association
PO Box 302
Orpington
Kent BR6 8QX
Telephone: 01689 850227
Web site: www.sfla.org.uk

UK College of Family Mediators
Alexander House
Telephone Avenue
Bristol BS1 4BS
Telephone: 0117 904 7223
Web site: www.ukcfm.co.uk

Victim Support
Telephone: 0845 3030 900

Women's Aid National Domestic Violence Helpline
Helpline: 08457 023468
Web site: www.womensaid.org.uk

Quick-reference Helplines	
Child Support Agency National Enquiry Line	08457 133 133
Children's Legal Centre	01206 873820
Community Legal Service Helpline	0845 608 1122
Gingerbread	0800 018 4318
NSPCC	0800 800 5000
One Parent Families	0800 018 5026
Parentline Plus	0808 800 2222
Refuge 24-hour Domestic Violence Helpline	08705 995443
Samaritans	08457 909090
Victim Support	0845 3030 900
Women's Aid National Domestic Violence Helpline	08457 023468

INDEX

Page numbers in **bold** indicate major references

absent parents 180
  see also contact
access *see* contact
Acknowledgement of Service 18–19, 44, **56–57**, 180
  respondent ignores 59
adultery 12–13, 27, **44–46**, 55, 147–148, 180
  proving 44, 45
  refusal to acknowledge 19–20, 25, **45–46**
  void after 6 months 45–46
ancillary relief 88, 180
Application for Ancillary Relief 88
assets **73–74**, 182
  and cohabiting 16, 32
  compensation money 100
  court settlements 79–83
  disclosure of 20–22, 28–29
  disposal of before settlement 100
  factors affecting settlements 79–83
  inheritances 99–100
  Schedule of Assets 75
  sharing of 17–18, 73–74
  splitting equally 14–15, 28, 80
  see also finances; houses
Attachment of Earnings Order 180

balance of harm tests 127
barristers **38–39**, 180
beneficial interest 134
benefits, State 75–76, **137–144**
  information sources 140
Budgeting Loans 141

Calderbank Offers **97–98**, 180
capitalising maintenance 101
cash equivalent transfer value (CETV) 29, 75
Certificate of Entitlement to a decree 57
Child Benefit 139, 184
Child Maintenance *see* Child Support
Child Support 31, **143–144**
  and access 14
  and cohabiting 135
Child Support Agency 31–32, 77, 135, **143–144**, 180, 184

Child Tax Credit 75–76, **139**
children 103–120
  abused 152
  access (absent parents) 13–14, 25–26, 30, 115, 116–117
  access (new partners) 14
  of cohabiting parents 131–132
  court orders 106–120
  and domestic violence 27, 30, 115
  helping during divorce 119–120
  Statement of Arrangements for 55, 57, **103–106**, 183
  see also contact; residence
Children's Legal Centre 184
clean break 30, 101, 180
  Clean Break Orders 79
co-respondents 45, 55, 180
cohabiting 131–135
  after divorce 77
  before divorce 16, 32
  and children 131–132
  and domestic violence 135
  and financial settlements 132–135
  and maintenance 134–135
common law marriage *see* cohabiting
Community Care Grants 141
Community Legal Service 70, 184
compensation money as an asset 100
con 38, 180
Consent Orders 181
contact 13–14, 25–26, 150–151, 180, 186
  arrangements 25–26, **115–119**
  case studies 155
Contact Orders 30, 118, 119
court proceedings 117–119
  direct 118
  indirect 119
contested divorce 60
costs 23–24, 40
  court costs 97–98
Council Tax Benefit 142
counsels *see* barristers
counselling 36, 185
  domestic violence 122, 123
court hearings 38–39
court orders 76–79
court proceedings
  contact 117–119
  financial matters 87–97

length of 13, 24
necessity of 26
court settlements 79–83
Crisis Loans 141
cross decrees 60
cross-petitions 60
custody *see* residence

debts 15
decrees
cross decrees 60
decree absolute 58, 181
decree nisi 57, 65, 181
defending a divorce 25, 48–49, 56,
59–60
desertion **50–51**, 181
directions for trial 56–57
Disability Living Allowance 142
disclosure 20–22, 28–29
divorce
after first year 44
conduct of 48
contested 60
England and Wales 58
grounds for 10, 26–27, **43–51**
length of 13, 24
myths 9–22
stages of 53–60
without a solicitor 53
divorce petitions 24–25, **55**, 181
cross-petitions 60
example of 61–64
domestic violence 121–130
case studies 159–169
and children 27, 30, 115
and cohabitation 135
helplines 122, 123
legal position 123–130
perpetrators of 122
victims of 121–122

emotional abuse 47
see also domestic violence;
unreasonable behaviour
enforcement proceedings 181
equity 181
ex parte orders 124

Families Need Fathers 184
family court advisers 26, **108–111**, 181
Family Crisis Centres 122
Family Law Act (1996) 135
Family Mediators Association 185

fathers *see* absent parents; contact;
residence
fees *see* costs
Final Hearing 94–97
finances
case studies 154–155
of cohabiting couples 132–135
court orders 76–79
court process 87–97
court settlements 79–83
disclosure of 20–22, 28–29
disposal of before settlement 100
factors affecting settlements 79–83
foreign accounts 28–29
gathering information about 72
importance of advice 72–73
see also assets; grants; loans
Financial Dispute Resolution Hearing
90–94, 181
First Appointment 88, 89–90

Gingerbread 185
grants 141
grounds for divorce 10, 26–27, **43–51**

habitually resident 182
*Handbook of the UK college of Family
Mediators* 69
health costs and benefits 138
helplines 188
domestic violence 122, 123
houses (marital homes) 83–87
and cohabiting 16, 32, 133–134
equity 181
Mesher Orders 78
Orders for Sale 78–79
ownership of 98
registering your interest 99
sharing 10–11, 17–18, 27–28,
83–87
Housing Benefit 142

Incapacity Benefit 137, **142–143**
Income Support 138
inferences about financial
information 20–21
inheritances as assets 99–100
injunctions *see* Non-molestation
Orders
Interim Orders 182

Jobseeker's Allowance 137–138
Joint Residence Orders 114–115

Law Society of England and Wales 185
legal advice 27
    see also barristers; solicitors
Legal Aid 15–16, 34, 40–41
    calculating 41
    for mediation 68
Legal Aid Franchise 16, 34, 41, 182
Legal help and Help at Court 40–41
Legal Services Commission 182, 185
living together see cohabiting
loans 141
London Marriage Guidance 185
Lump Sum Orders 77

maintenance 182
    capitalising 101
    children 31, 77–78, 135, **143–144**
    and cohabiting 134–135
    ex spouse 30–31, 77, 134, 150
Maintenance Pending Suits 76, 182
marriage
    difficulty leaving 146–147, 154
    equal contributions to 17–18
    guidance 185, 187
matrimonial assets see assets
mediation **67–70**, 182, 185, 186, 188
Mesher Order 78
money see assets; finances

National Association of Child Contact
    Centres 186
National Council for One Parent
    Families 186
National Family and Parenting
    Institute 186
National Family Mediation 70, 186
Non-molestation Orders 123,
    124–126, 182
NSPCC 185

Occupation Orders 123, **126–130**,
    182
    and ownership 129–130
One Parent Families 186
Orders for Sale 78–79

papers, refusal to sign 18–19, 24–25
parental responsibility **131–132**, 182
Parentline Plus 186–187
parents see absent parents; contact;
    residence
partners, new 14
PDT Family Mediators 186

pensions
    Pension Sharing Orders 79
    sharing of 11–12, 29
Periodical Payments Order 77–78
    see also maintenance
perpetration hearings 109–111
petitioners 24, 55, 58, 183
petitions 24–25, **55**, 181
    cross-petitions 60
    example of 61–64
power of arrest 125
pre-action protocol 88
Principal Registry of the Family
    Division 187
Prohibited Steps Orders **119**, 183
property see houses
Property Adjustment Orders **78**, 183

Refuge helpline 123, 187
refuges 122–123
refusal
    to agree to divorce 19–20, 24–25
    to sign papers 18–19
Relate 187
remarriage
    and maintenance 31–32, 77
residence 106, 107–115
    applications 107–108
    children's views 113
    factors deciding 112–113
    final hearing 111–112
    joint residence 114–115
    reapplying for 114
Residence Orders **113**, 183
respondents 58, **58–59**, 183
    defending the divorce 25, 48–49,
        56, **59–60**
    non-cooperation of 59
    Notice of Proceedings to 56
Reunite 187

Samaritans 187
savings, individual 15
Schedule of Assets 75
separation **49–50**, 183
settlement, court 79–83
Social Fund 141
solicitors 27, 183
    and barristers 38–39
    choosing 15–16, 33–35
    communicating with 37–38
    first meeting with 33, **35–36**, 54
    franchised 16, 34, 411

role of 37
  see also costs
Solicitors' Family Law Association 34, 187
Special Procedure List 56–57
Specific Issue Orders **119**, 183
spouses 183
  non-working 17–18
State benefits 75–76, **137–144**
  information sources 140
Statement of Arrangements for the Children 55, 57, **103–106**, 183

UK College of Family Mediators 188
undertakings **126**, 183
unfaithfulness 12–13, 27
  see also adultery

unreasonable behaviour 19–20, 45–46, **46–49**, 183
  case studies 149, 153–159, 173–174
  example of 64
  refusal to acknowledge 48–49
  see also domestic violence

Victim Support 188
violence, see domestic violence

welfare checklist **112–113**, 183
wives, non-working 17–18
Women's Aid 122, 188
women's refuges 122–123
Working Families' Tax Credit 139
Working Tax Credit 75–76, **140**